Feral Self-Care

100 Ways to Liberate and Celebrate Your Messy, Wild, and Untamed Self

MANDI EM

Author of *Witchcraft Therapy*

ADAMS MEDIA

NEW YORK LONDON TORONTO SYDNEY NEW DELHI

Aadams media

Adams Media
An Imprint of Simon & Schuster, Inc.
100 Technology Center Drive
Stoughton, Massachusetts 02072

First Adams Media hardcover edition October 2023

ADAMS MEDIA and colophon are registered trademarks of Simon & Schuster, Inc.

For information about special discounts for bulk purchases, please contact Simon & Schuster Special Sales at 1-866-506-1949 or business@simonandschuster.com.

The Simon & Schuster Speakers Bureau can bring authors to your live event. For more information or to book an event, contact the Simon & Schuster Speakers Bureau at 1-866-248-3049 or visit our website at www.simonspeakers.com.

Interior design by Sylvia McArdle
Hand lettering by Priscilla Yuen
Interior images © 123RF; Getty Images; Simon & Schuster, Inc.

Manufactured in the United States of America

1 2023

Library of Congress Cataloging-in-Publication Data
Names: Em, Mandi, author.
Title: Feral self-care / Mandi Em, author of Witchcraft therapy.
Description: First Adams Media hardcover edition. | Stoughton, Massachusetts: Adams Media, 2023
Identifiers: LCCN 2023019630 | ISBN 9781507221372 (hc) | ISBN 9781507221389 (ebook)
Subjects: LCSH: Self-help techniques. | Well-being.
Classification: LCC BF632 .E65 2023 | DDC 158.1--dc23/eng/20230616
LC record available at https://lccn.loc.gov/2023019630

ISBN 978-1-5072-2137-2
ISBN 978-1-5072-2138-9 (ebook)

CONTENTS

Introduction

Self-care has become a booming industry for good reason: Many of us wander through life feeling tired, distracted, and energetically tapped out. But sadly, the solutions we're given seem to reek of the same blush pink bullshit and consumerism that got us to a place of running on fumes in the first place. So what's a person gotta do to get a little self-care on when they're emotionally drained and more apt to *throw* a bath bomb than relax with one?

Feral self-care!

Feral self-care is a rejection of the idea that self-care can be bought or obtained through picture-perfect methods. It is digging into the here and now to find peace and fulfillment in the messy reality of where you're at. It's about connecting with your body, chaos, and nature to return to a state of primal, zero-fucks-given energy as a route to wellness! And the best part is that it doesn't require any tools or outside participation for your own healing. *Feral Self-Care* is loaded with uniquely wild self-care tips and practices that will actually help you nourish your soul and feel good. No yoga. No spa days. Just some truly unhinged fun that is good for your wellness (despite potentially making the neighbors worry about your sanity).

Here you'll find one hundred activities to serve as inspiration for living your best untamed life. You'll:

- Get wild, like tuning in to the cycles of nature and dancing in the rain.
- Tap into all your senses, like lazing in sunbeams and getting messy with food.
- Embrace chaos and creativity, like making a blanket fort and creating unhinged affirmations.
- Muck around in the inner swamp of the self, like leaning into lazy and brawling with your inner critic.
- Connect with your feral community, like engaging in co-creation and feasting with loved ones.
- And express your unruly spiritual side, like making a date with your intuition and creating a sacred space.

In embracing feral self-care, you will feel more empowered, free, and confident in this human experience and all its messy glory. So say goodbye to domestication; it's time to go feral!

How to Use This Book

This book is meant to not only be read but to be *experienced*. The entries within give unique, bordering on unruly, self-care strategies. In keeping with the feral self-care ethos, you're gonna have to *feel* it to believe it.

Each entry will cover an idea that marries one self-care concept with a primal need that it fulfills, such as going barefoot to reconnect with the earth and finding your flow as an accessible alternative to traditional meditation. The benefits will be felt in every aspect of life, from your mental health and spirituality to your relationships and how you authentically express yourself. The concepts and strategies explored are meant to strip the restrictive trappings of what is "acceptable" in modern society and help you lean into little moments that honor the unruly creature within—the human mammal! The inner child! The feral gremlin within you that pulls on the periphery of your awareness and yearns to be free! When reading this book, feel free to jump around to the entries that pique your interest, as there is no particular order needed to get the full benefit of these practices. Each will serve as inspiration and guidance for liberating your unique, authentic, untamed self.

As you move through the entries, you can keep track of whether any bring up some internal resistance and explore why these ideas or practices may feel challenging. You can even pair this guide with a journal to reflect on your experiences and record any insights that come up. In many cases, the conditioning we get from childhood to "sit down, stay small, be quiet, fit in, make nice" can act as a barrier to embrace our full potential to live our best unhinged life. However, many barriers are meant to be broken, and break them we shall! Feel free to embrace the messy spirit of feral self-care as you work with this book: Underline your favorite bits, dog-ear the pages, scribble notes in the margins. This is a wonderfully chaotic journey to celebrate and liberate your wildest self. Have fun and don't waste time worrying about the "right" or "acceptable" way to do anything. Let's get feral!

CHAPTER 1

What Does It Mean to Go Feral?

Going feral is embracing your animal nature and honoring your primal instincts. It is accepting and owning your unique authenticity even if it doesn't quite fit in with prevailing societal norms. It is understanding that you are always primally perfect in all of your messy, chaotic glory. To go feral is to embrace the many dimensions of your *wild*! And wild is what people once were. Prior to civilization as it is now known, human beings lived in tandem with nature, following their instincts, and not yet influenced by the kind of large-scale societal and cultural conditioning that's present in the modern age. However, through the years of advancing technologies, industrialization, etc., humans have become domesticated. This isn't necessarily a bad thing—in fact, in doing so, our species has thrived in many ways. Yet despite domestication there is still a deep-seated urge that tugs at the edges of our awareness. The wild longing to be freed from the constraints of modern life. In making space to honor this primal nature, you tap into a wellspring of self-care, freeing up valuable energy that would have you putting a lid on authentic expression, and allowing yourself to find liberation in letting your wild nature come out and play.

In this chapter, you will learn more about the ethos of feral self-care and how this system of wellness can inform your self-care practices so that you approach life in a way that's authentic and free. While you may not be ditching your pants and sprinting into the woods just yet, the foundational concepts in this chapter will help you make the most of the freeing practices found later in this book and challenge your ideas of traditional wellness and self-care going forward.

HONORING THE URGE TO GO FERAL: FOUNDATIONAL PRINCIPLES OF FERAL SELF-CARE

Feral self-care is an approach to wellness that shucks off the dusty, uptight restrictions of what it means to be a modern, civilized human in favor of living more aligned with our true animal nature. Honoring the urge to go feral means intentionally making space in our lives to liberate and celebrate those messy and chaotic aspects of ourselves and embracing the compelling call of the wild as an antidote to modern-day pressures.

The following foundational principles that form the heart of the feral self-care ethos help you do just that.

Connecting with Nature

What is wild if not wilderness itself? Part of going feral is to embrace nature—both the natural environment and your *own* animal nature. The human mammal is *of* nature, and indeed, you are born as naked and free from civilization as any other creature!

When you cultivate a relationship with the earth and nature itself, you can become a student of all the lessons it has to offer. You can learn about patience, about connection, and about what it means to make the most of being a creature of this planet—all of which lead to feeling happier, healthier, and whole.

Embracing the Sensory Portal of Your Body

In our wild, untamed nature, our experience of the world is a felt one. The body is the vessel with which we encounter and interpret the world. These experiences are a symphony played by the five senses: There is pleasure, pain, and everything in between. Often, our minds can be so full of endless thought loops and imagined bullshit scenarios that we find ourselves disconnected from the wisdom of our animal bodies. It becomes easy to forget about all the things our senses are taking in right this moment. Instead of mindfully tuning in to the present, we get stuck in the past or future.

When you turn your awareness back to your physical sensations, you can return to the restorative state of simply *being*. A state separate from the expectations and obligations of civilized modern life. Embrace your feral self by allowing the sensations of your life to form a blanket of self-care that will pull you out of your mind and into your body.

Weaving Chaos

Another fundamental aspect of going feral is to recognize that life is inherently chaotic and unpredictable at times and that by trying to fight this fact, you are actually missing out on opportunities. For people, so masterful at making the environment suit *them,* to accept and even (gasp!) embrace chaos is to make themselves available to learn resilience in action. *This* is how you "weave" chaos, or take the wildly unpredictable mess you are given and direct it into the shape of your choosing. Something productive and valuable. To weave chaos is to align with the natural order of things and to embrace the many lessons and possibilities that follow.

Embracing Creativity and Play

You can weave chaos through creativity. As a human being, it is in your nature to be deeply creative—and artistic talent (or lack thereof) has nothing to do with it. Creativity is simply a dimension of the human experience, and you can tap into its brilliance whether you're feeling artsy, solving problems, or simply dreaming up what could happen next. Your ancestors flexed their creative muscles when tasked with interpreting the world around them, and you can see this in their art, spirituality, and symbolism. In contrast, the modern era has seen a decline in this sort of messy, intuitive interpretation in favor of logic and science. When going feral you must embrace that chaotic, creative critter that lies within, and give it an outlet through messy play and a return to spirit and symbol. There is a lot of satisfying self-care to be found in inviting this kind of chaos into your life.

Navigating the Inner Swamp

Part of going feral is not to just tromp around in the swamps *out there* but to fully explore the swamp *within yourself*. The human being is a creature that has murky depths, and the human experience is one that is full of triumphs, tribulations, glory, pain, and everything in between. This messiness can feel difficult at times for many to hold. In addition to this, the rise of media (especially social media) has perpetuated this idea that your life "should" be a lot shinier and tidier than it is. The real truth is that we are all out here just winging it and doing our best.

This notion that you aren't quite getting it "right" is crap, I tell ya! You must reject the urge to gloss over the hard stuff, as it's in the depths of your own messy swamp that you can find true healing and self-care.

Cultivating Community

We are social creatures, and so any discussion of embracing our true, feral nature would not be complete without talking about our relations to one another. Our species has evolved through community, and there is so much healing and self-care we can find through community still. As part of the feral self-care ethos, we must remember that our relationships with one another can fulfill primal needs we have for love and belonging. In cultivating community, we can not only find our own inner wellness but begin to weave a tapestry of wild connection throughout social networks.

Acknowledging Spirit

Human beings are spiritual in nature. Although we may not vibe with religion, we still have deep and primal needs for spiritual fulfillment.

Sadly, our modern society is not one that emphasizes the importance of spiritual development as a form of self-care. In fact, the spiritual dimension of life can be dismissed completely and sometimes even belittled. If you don't have a religious or mystical worldview, there is a greater chance that this dimension of your nature may be longing for the chance to be acknowledged and expressed. The impacts of neglecting spiritual care can be seen all around, as many people feel hopeless and unfulfilled in today's busy, production-focused world. In once again acknowledging the role of spirit in your wild and primal nature, you can connect with guidance, purpose, and meaning. Again, it's important to note that a religious worldview is not necessary for this dimension of humanity to be expressed. You can do it through symbol, ritual, and truly connecting with a primal sense of wonder and awe.

RADICALLY ACCEPTING THE UNHINGED PARTS OF YOURSELF

One of the most insidious aspects of modern civilization is the tendency to mute yourself for the sake of fitting in. Look, there is no rule book on how you have to show up to your life. And a lot of the urge to throttle self-expression is based on assumptions. Assumptions that you will be criticized and even rejected by others. And to be honest, that may happen sometimes, but it's a risk that is *vastly* outweighed by the freedom and happiness that comes with being true to who you are.

As you start practicing feral self-care, you will need to radically accept all the uncultivated and messy aspects of yourself—and fold them into your outward expression if it feels good to do so. In your wildest state, self-expression comes naturally and is aligned with spirit and impulse and backed by a desire to only please yourself. You are brilliantly unique! It's time to embrace it! Let feral self-care be a living love letter to the wild, untamed creature within.

CHAPTER 2

Cozying Up to Mother Nature:

REWILDING FOR WELLNESS

As a member of the human species, deep within your spirit is an unruly woodland creature that seeks the connection and grounding that comes from bonding with the land. Although humans have over time disconnected from nature in terms of where we live, how we obtain food, and how we spend our leisure time, this hasn't necessarily been a positive shift when it comes to the overall wellness of our species. Nurturing a connection with nature can give some much-needed relief from the pressures of modern existence. You can gain precious perspective and a lot of self-care through plugging back into this larger system in which you belong. For example, many of the modern problems that plague our awareness in an urban existence seem trivial at the foot of a sunset or other humbling natural phenomena. Nature is a restorative reminder that this industrial world is not all there is to life and that you are part of a vast cosmos!

In this chapter, you will get wild in nature through practices like skygazing and foraging. As a human creature, reclaim your birthright through rewilding yourself—a particularly potent source of wellness in a modern landscape that leaves most feeling lost and disconnected.

Follow Nature's Cycles

Any discussion of going feral must first be planted in the awareness of where you stand in the natural order of things. Humans are animals, yet ones that don't quite fit into nature like other animals do. You can see evidence of this all around you when looking at the impact and control people have had over the environment. No other mammal has managed to throw its weight around so obnoxiously and create such a separation between themselves and nature. Despite this advantageous-yet-somewhat-backward "progress," the domestication of humans has left a longing deep in your primal little spirit, and there is much to be gained by reclaiming your wild!

There is a natural rhythm and order to things that you probably don't look to for comfort nearly enough in the hustle of the everyday grind. The cycles of the stars, the seasons, and even the alternation of day and night are very important rhythms people tend to take for granted in modern life. These cycles and patterns once guided humans; however, you can turn away from them thanks to 24/7 lighting, heating and AC, and a variety of other artificial comforts that keep you truckin' regardless of what's going on outside.

To go feral is to tune back in, baby! Your very first feral self-care assignment is this: Reconnect with the cycles of nature. Align yourself with the natural rhythms around you as a way to rewild your primal human spirit. Observe the cycles of the earth around you, of the sky and the cosmos, and of time and the seasons. As lost as you may feel at times, you are truly steeped in guidance and lessons communicated to you through these cycles. Once familiar with them, you may be able to approach life more easily, supported by the natural order of things.

How to Do It

1. The first step is to learn and observe. What are the cycles of nature in your local regions and in your life? For instance, are there distinct seasons? Temperature or environmental shifts that influence the region? Are there shifts in plant or wildlife activity that you can observe or learn from?

2. Next, think about the ways you might be forcing yourself to *counter* these cycles. For example, in the wild many animals hibernate or lower their energetic output in winter or in poor conditions. However, in human society we are expected to be just as productive and gung ho across every season. Are there ways that your life is set up to have you working against your "creature clock"?

3. Finally, find ways to work *with* these cycles, and use them for guidance. For example, if you tend to have the urge to reduce your energy in the colder months (much like the plants and animals in the wild), maybe this would be a good time to focus on restorative and cozy self-care that would otherwise be pushed to the bottom of your to-do list rather than focus on forcing yourself to tackle new projects and goals.

You gain a lot from this task. What can you learn from these rhythms? What can they tell you about yourself and about life itself? That there is a time to play and a time to rest? That hard work pays off? That there are seasons for *everything*? That everything has its time and that comfort and predictability are not always guaranteed? 'Tis the way of the wild!

By looking to where you belong in nature and recognizing that you are but one piece of a larger whole, you initiate the path to feral self-care. You can be soothed and guided by the wild out there. In doing so, you reclaim your place in the natural order of things.

Get Back to Barefoot

Maybe it's an unpopular opinion, but shoes are by far one of the most obnoxious articles of clothing there are. It doesn't matter if it's Crocs or Gucci loafers—anything that keeps the mud, sand, grass, and sweet, energetic vapors of Mother Earth from making a home in between your toes is a missed opportunity for some primal, feral fun!

In the modern age, there's an ever-present disconnection that can feel immensely isolating. Most domesticated humans are isolated from themselves, from the natural world, and from the simple, earthy delights of our animal nature. Shoes are but one example of this disconnect, a symbol of our distance from our free-footed mammalian nature.

It's time to reconnect!

There is an immense amount of joy and pleasure that comes from sinking your bare feet into the many sensory surfaces of nature as a form of self-care. The feral critter inside you delights every time you let the waves wash over your toes, run through the grass, and kiss the soil through the soles of your feet! This satisfies a deep and primal itch, as your untamed animal nature longs to frolic freely on this beautiful planet that you get to call home.

Grounding (also referred to as "earthing") is the practice of electrically "co-regulating" yourself by connecting the electrical field of your body to the electrical field of the earth. Although there is research that supports the physical and mental health benefits of these practices, the felt experience of mindfully touching your feet to the ground is profoundly healing in and of itself. Essentially, those who try it, *get it.*

When you indulge the natural urges you have to kick off your shoes and experience the grounding presence of the earth, you establish an energetic "cord" that sends currents of primal magic back and forth between your body and the planet itself. It's time to banish your shoes and socks and get those feet dirty! *Literally!* Get back to barefoot as a way to experience some feral self-care.

How to Do It

1. Say "*fuck no*" to shoes. Get outside and squelch in the mud, stir your toes in the sand, or garden barefoot.
2. As you do so, take deep, cleansing breaths (inhale through your nose and exhale through your mouth), and pay close attention to how your body feels during this grounding practice. After all, this is a felt experience and one that can bring up many delightful and primal tactile sensations.

As you feel the earth between your toes, quiet your mind and sink into the joy of being an untamed cosmic creature that is connecting to this wild and wonderful planet.

Indulge that primal need you have to sink into the experience of the earth beneath your feet. Indulge that wild critter within by releasing yourself from modern domestication, one shoe at a time. Get back on your barefoot bullshit!

Hug a Tree (Literally)

Media is full of the "tree hugger" trope: an unimaginative dismissal of "tree hugging" as being some sort of flaky hippie pastime. However, dismissing it as such sounds like just the sort of thing someone who could use a tree hug would do. What, you *don't* want to feel the rough, papery kiss of bark against your cheek? Or the embrace of a stable elder?

In all seriousness, tree hugging is a felt experience that can be deeply nurturing and fulfilling. Trees are not inanimate objects, you know this, yet there is an illusion out there that their "aliveness" isn't as active as a human's due to a misunderstanding of scale. Their life cycle and the things they "do" sprawls on a different timeline than our own, so it is easy to dismiss the potential sentience or spirit of trees. But although they do not move, speak, or yield to the touch in the same ways we do as humans, this is not to imply that they are without soul or life. Actually, they are vibrantly full of nourishing energy. Finding comfort in the (one-sided) embrace of one of these beauties is a top-tier experience. Once you get past the post-civilization awkwardness of initiating the hug (the ball is all in your court, baby), you may find yourself having an emotional experience you didn't expect. Indeed, trees could teach humans a thing or two, as they engage in social behaviors such as nutrient sharing and sending underground signals through underground networks to their surroundings. Although they do not communicate and respond to the world in the way that we've typically recognized as sentient, they are quickly teaching us to expand our ideas.

They also don't talk back and are phenomenal listeners!

To take a moment to appreciate the "aliveness" of trees is to fundamentally broaden your understanding of the things in nature that deserve your reverence and respect. To hug a tree (literally) is humbling, gives perspective, and helps you tap into the feral woods goblin inside you that knows damn well that trees are *definitely* better than people.

So your next feral self-care assignment is this: Go hug a tree!

How to Do It

If you're wondering where to start, the following is a good guideline for initiating this sort of interspecies cuddle:

1. Find a tree that "calls" to you (when you know, you know!).
2. Open your arms and calmly approach the tree. Ask for consent. Make note of the "answer" (this will likely be an intuitive felt sense or environmental cue).
3. Check the tree for potential hazards (sap, sharp branches, creepy-crawlies), then initiate a hug!
4. As you hug the tree, take deep breaths and allow your energy field to comingle with the energy field of the tree and the itty-bitty ecosystems it contains.
5. Have a big, relaxing sigh or a wee cry or a laugh if needed.
6. Thank the tree!

After you try this out, make note of how it made you feel. Was it an emotional experience? Did it help make your problems melt away for the moment? What sensations were present in your animal body both during and after the experience?

This is an important reminder that self-care is not always something to be bought or sold. Sometimes self-care is as simple as tapping into the natural world as a balm for the chapped modern soul.

Drop Out of Consumerist Culture

A hallmark of the modern age is an unprecedented access to *stuff*. In Western society you're no longer required to forage, hunt, and create things by hand to serve your needs. The entire concept of things that are "built to last" seems to be a thing of the past. There is an absolutely bonkers amount of stuff that you can amass in your life, and all of it feels very important despite the fact that humanity adapted for ages without any of this shit. What's worse is that we live in a disposable culture, where for the most part we are able to use things for a short time then throw them away, essentially getting to a place where we constantly replace stuff with...*more* stuff!

Although the convenience of such a scenario can't be argued, it is having a lasting impact not only on the human species but on everything else on this planet. As people have strayed from human nature and nature itself, the species has gotten to a place of not only dominating the planet but disrespectfully trampling it with very little care for the ecosystem or even future generations. Industries, societies, and culture seem to be built on chasing profit rather than delivering goods.

If you take a step back, it becomes crystal clear that not only is this way unsustainable, but you don't really need to be caught up in this in the first place. This isn't to say you should never buy anything again but that everyone could stand to look critically at this disposable culture and ask themselves if they really need all of this stuff. On a primal level, people need the things that help them survive and thrive, and all this other stuff is just window dressing to fit in with modern consumer society.

Your feral self-care task will focus on looking at alternatives to participating in this system. Try to find ways to repurpose or reuse old goods, turning trash into treasure! This can be a powerful act of self-care as it allows you to get back to basics and explore how much you actually *want* to play along with the modern system. With a little ingenuity, you can reclaim your wild by distancing yourself from consumerist culture one small step at a time.

How to Do It

To distance yourself from consumerist culture, start by looking at your problems and needs. Is there a way you can still get what you need without spending money? Is there another use for the things that you were originally going to throw out?

Some simple suggestions of things you can do to start breaking your ties with consumerist culture include:

- **Foraging or creating items that you need:** For example, making DIY body-care products, foraging for food or decor, and making or mending your own clothes.
- **Repurposing items:** Repurposing, or "upcycling," is when you take an item, typically something that is broken or you no longer have use for, and figure out a new, creative use for it. To repurpose things is not only an environmentally friendly act but an act of self-care for your expressive inner goblin!
- **Participating in "trade economies":** Maybe you have a skill or talent that can be used in trades for the things or services you require? For example, if you are good at knitting, can you make a sweater in trade for some other needed item? This kind of economy was key in human societies in the past.

However you choose to tackle this, just know that every small step counts, both for the planet and for your own self-care.

Listen to the Land

Just because humans and the land communicate differently doesn't imply a lack of communication entirely. You are given clues; all around you nature is brimming with signs and messages that, if observed, can help you thrive and allow you to live as an ally and friend to the land. Whether it be signs of impending seasonal shifts, such as falling leaves or flowers in bloom; balances/imbalances in wildlife activity, such as the sudden halt of birdsong that may occur when a storm is approaching; or other subtle clues, such as scents or subtle electrical shifts that can be felt in the breeze, there is much you can learn by paying attention to your natural surroundings.

In most cases it is a matter of literacy that acts as a barrier. Prior to the modern era of TV screens and the ability to live comfortably apart from the land, people were required to speak the language of the land in order to be successful. For example, learning which environmental or wildlife cues indicated a lurking predator or paying keen attention to natural indicators of impending weather shifts. In rural areas and in many cultures around the world, this is still the case. However, for many in Western and/or less rural environments, this back and forth with the land is sorely missing.

Although it's unlikely that in urban culture people will have a full return to the kind of reciprocal relationship between humans and the land that was once enjoyed, there is still much to be gained from mindfully working to bridge this gap with knowledge and observation. As you improve your communication with nature, you can reap the fulfillment and benefits that come from being able to read nature's cues, from helping in simple things, like making adequate preparations for weather, to more serious applications, such as ensuring safety in the event of a survival situation. After all, it doesn't matter how big the wall we humans build between ourselves and nature is: There will always be a place for this knowledge in order for our species to truly thrive. If somehow the comforts of modernity were pulled out from under you, this kind of knowledge would likely save your ass!

So learn to listen to the land as an act of feral self-care. It will not only make you feel more grounded and connected, but building this relationship can be a powerful resource.

How to Do It

To commune with nature starts with learning its language. This requires observance. Pay attention to the land and take notes about what you witness. What does it look like when the seasons change and shift? What succession can you witness in plant and insect life over the course of a day? Of a week? A month and year? How does the weather play a role in the shifts and cycles of nature? What patterns can you find? Can you gain some helpful perspective about what it means to be a humble creature of this planet?

As you note things about the land, task yourself to learn from books, groups, or more experienced humans to tie this information together. Improving your "literacy" in regard to nature (a.k.a. bioliteracy) can be an incredibly fulfilling way to indulge the call of the wild and go feral. You can learn and gather information from what you can see and witness through your own senses and also from the insights, observations, and wisdom others have gathered in their own journey to communicate with the land.

Revel in the Beauty of Dead Things

Sometimes self-care comes in the form of observance and finding the lesson in something that can be integrated into your own life. Being a person is *fucking hard*, but often the multitude of stressors and anxieties you face can all be boiled down to a few simple lessons: Everything has its season, you must get comfortable with discomfort, and things are constantly cycling (every ending is a beginning in disguise).

In modern society, and particularly Western culture, people tend to be uncomfortable with grief, death, and endings of all sorts. They hold it away from themselves, giving it distance, which doesn't really help them to acclimatize to the experience. Death is a fundamental part of life after all, and there are many things you can learn when you begin to accept its place in the larger order of things.

I personally have a summer goblin spirit that delights in lazy lake days and long sunny hikes with loads of pretty plants to gaze at. I've always found myself emotionally wintering (pulling inward and somewhat "wilting" in energy and enthusiasm) in the colder months, and it wasn't until I began to soak up the beauty of dead things that I found myself more resilient to life's seasons and changes. By finding the beauty in dead things, you can find a reminder that some are seasons for living and that some are for resting. That some beautiful things are not for keeps and instead hold space temporarily for other things to come. And that there is always a time for everything. Even death.

So reject the shiny illusion that anything lasts in perpetuity! Real life is gritty, messy, and tinged with joy and grief in equal measures. *This* is what it is to be alive! Find feral self-care in recognizing that all things must end but that the sadness and discomfort that comes with this fact is also accompanied by a hope and resilience that can be deeply rejuvenating. Find the beauty in dead things—wilted leaves, old bones, and the shell of something that has passed. Take in the lesson: Everything has its time to bloom and wither, an enduring loop of what it is to be alive!

How to Do It

1. To find the beauty in dead things, go out for a walk during the liminal space between seasons, particularly in the fall. This works best if you choose a path or trail that you've already walked during the lusher, more abundant months. Then you already hold a mental picture of what it was like before things became sparser.
2. During your walk, take note of the beauty of the plants dying, the leaves dropping, and the decay of the previously lush flora. All of this withering is what feeds and forms the foundation for new growth in the future.
3. Take note of what remains living (such as evergreen species) and what other aspects of the environment (bugs, lichens, mushrooms, etc.) you can see more clearly now due to the shift in growth.
4. As you observe your surroundings, take deep breaths, and remind yourself of the cyclical nature of life. That every ending is making way for something else.

One of the best lessons you can truly get through your skull that will have you brimming with resilience is that all shit ends, and new shit begins! This knowledge can help you swallow the discomfort and grief of most situations in favor of the quiet stillness of knowing that it's all gonna be all right.

Forage and Frolic

Humans and foraging go hand in hand. After all, foraging is the act of living off the land, something that people excelled at prior to the age of modern, civilized convenience. Indeed, the earth has many treasures available to those that seek them out, and humans were able to thrive for ages by gathering food, medicines, and items they could fashion into solving their problems. Sadly, the greed and disconnection of the modern age has strained this relationship with nature, and many people, especially those in urban settings, may never experience the feral fun of a good ol' fashioned forage!

To forage is to gather usable natural items that can be used to sustain your body or your lifestyle. In the age of 24/7 delivery and online shopping, foraging is like a little rebellion. A callback to your ancestors' hunter-gatherer ways. It is an act of feral self-care because it speaks to your primal nature, deepens your ties to nature, and even if you come back with nothing, you'll have gained valuable knowledge while embarking on this adventure. There is something very wild and powerful about gaining knowledge that can help you heal and care for yourself. You get that rugged, hairy-chest satisfaction that comes with self-sufficiency. Humans thrive on a sense of purpose, and there is a lot to be found through fending for yourself—especially when it means you also get to frolic in the woods like a goblin on a side quest.

So your next feral self-care suggestion is this: Learn to forage... even just a little. Whether it be for food, craft-making, or even just to learn, you may find yourself loving the act of taking to nature on a rewilding quest.

How to Do It

To get started, become familiar with what your local lands give. What are the native trees and plants? What role do they play in the local history or folklore of your region? How is their growth, appearance, and usefulness affected by the seasons in your area (for example, some plants look different in their first versus second year, or they are best harvested for use in particular seasons)? Are there any medicinal or functional uses of the plants in your area? Can they be harvested ethically?

A lot of this information can be found in books and field guides, as well as online; however, you can supercharge your learning by linking up with local foraging groups or asking experienced foragers for guidance. In many cases, foraging types are passionate about this knowledge and more than happy to pass it along (unless it's about valued mushroom-picking spots, in which case you might be met with some mystery!).

Foraging is not the sort of thing you learn in a single weekend. In many cases, to ensure that you proceed safely (especially when it comes to consumables) and ethically, you may spend years to get fully acquainted with the many stages of a particular plant across time and locations. Remember that it is not a race, and more knowledge is better at a slower pace than having half knowledge gained foolishly fast. By studying guides and learning hands-on from those more experienced, you can begin to gain a robust body of knowledge to help you on your endeavors.

Feral self-care is an exercise in moving beyond the bubble baths in favor of activities that will deeply satisfy those human urges to live in a more connected and purposeful way. Foraging (even if it's just to learn) can help you do just that.

Cozy Up to the Dark

One of the most understated yet dramatic differences between modern life and the lives of your ancestors is lighting. The near-constant illumination you now enjoy is a relatively recent phenomena for humans. Your ancestors cozied up to the dark, letting the cycles of natural light guide their lives, activities, and imaginations. Now, with access to electricity and around-the-clock light and entertainment, we humans have become more disconnected from the dark, something that may be impacting your health in sneaky ways.

There is a growing body of research on how the lack of darkness human beings now face affects our health and well-being. Your body's sleep-wake cycle is governed by something called a circadian rhythm, which is the cycle that gets you sleepy at night then jazzed to wake up in the morning. This rhythm is regulated by a hormone called melatonin, the production of which is influenced by—you guessed it—lighting! The interference of unnatural light through the twenty-four-hour sleep-wake cycle may be inducing physical and mental health detriments, such as hormonal imbalances, mood issues, and problems associated with disrupted sleep patterns.

All the more reason to embrace darkness as a form of feral self-care!

Aside from the potential physical health benefits, embracing darkness is a way you can soothe the primal parts of your spirit that long for a break from the bright and noisy chaos of modern society. This can be a powerful act of self-care—to allow yourself to just *be* in darkness, becoming enveloped in the feeling of the unknown. Ultimately, it is a profound act of surrender. When faced with your own thoughts in the absence of light, to vibe there for a while and let go of the need to control, is powerful.

Now, this isn't to suggest you should spend a night outside in a sketchy cave with only mysterious noises and the looming threat of the unknown as your companion. But it is wise to get your human reacquainted with the inky stillness of the night in safe, simple ways. To do so is deeply fulfilling for your animal nature, the part of you that longs to live in sync with the earth's natural cycles.

How to Do It

Turn off your devices, flick off the lights, and tune in to the darkness around you. Take deep breaths as you do.

If you want to give this task a rewilding boost, take it to a safe outdoor space. Begin by standing outside at night under the stars and simply take it all in: the calm, the dark, and the many sounds of nature's night shift. Indeed, you will find that the natural world is positively brimming with activity, although it may be more understated and mysterious than the bustle of the daytime hours. As you tune in to the dark, take time to breathe, and listen to the sounds around you. Inhale the scent of the night's air and take note of what you smell. What info can you gather in the dark? What games does your mind play to fill in the darkness? What would your surroundings have been like way back when things were wilder and less populated?

Cycles of light and dark are a part of your primal wiring. As a form of self-care, getting reacquainted with the dark is simple, costs nothing, and is likely to bring surprising rewards for both your physical and mental health.

Mud Paint

Play is a sadly underutilized yet primally necessary tool for self-care that doesn't seem to venture into adulthood. Remember the childhood joy of getting filthy outside, making your parents have a fit as you smeared your mud-stained hands along the wall? Childhood is defined by this kind of spontaneous, messy, imaginative play, and although it's something people grow out of doing, it's not something they grow out of *needing*.

What a joy it would be to embrace the unbridled, earthy fun of childhood in adulthood, where arguably you need it most. To freely indulge the urge to get messy in Mother Earth's playground! Watch any toddler on a spring day near mud puddles and you will see this impulse in action—splashing, finger painting in the dirt, and just generally finding joy in making a big ol' mess! Playing in the mud indulges some of your most primal urges to get messy, to play, to connect to nature, and to spontaneously create. As a form of self-care, to embrace these opportunities for messy outdoor play is a balm that your soul longs for in the halogen-lit, Lysol-treated kitchens of modern existence!

As you will learn more about in Chapter 4, inside your untamed depths is a feral creative spirit, even if you do not identify as an "artist." Creativity is fundamental to our human nature, but to liberate this creative part of yourself, you must release the idea that creation has to be palatable. That you must have all the pretty tools and shiny things to create in a way that's pleasing for the consumption of others. *Bullshit!*

Creation is an ever-present force that is always bubbling under the surface, waiting to be released in bursts of song, flailing limbs, and puddles of mud. And if we strip away the conditioning of our polite society, our very human selves can find so much joy and healing in messy, creative play. Particularly when we spontaneously indulge in using the gifts provided by nature. Self-care doesn't always have to have a price tag; you do not need to have all the right paints or store-bought tools. What can be even more deeply fulfilling is to use what's available in any given moment, allowing you to follow the impulse as it strikes and take those opportunities to connect with nature and play.

How to Do It

1. On the next warm day after it's rained, approach your nearest muddy puddle armed with paintbrushes, sticks, leaves, or even just your eager fingers!
2. Dip into the mud and begin to paint. Large boulders or smooth rocks work well as a canvas, although you can also use slabs of wood, bits of paper, conks, or a concrete sidewalk.
3. Follow your impulses: As with most things feral self-care, the more thought that goes in, the more magic is lost.

As for what you choose to paint, well, that's up to you! Emotive splatters, funny quotes, cave painting–style icons—there really are no rules here! Allow yourself the freedom to get messy. Lean into your intuitive urges as you allow your inner toddler to play, unleashing all the fun, mucky delight that can come with such a rejuvenating act of feral self-care.

Worship Your Wild

Throughout history, humankind has used spirituality as a way of interpreting and interfacing with the larger natural world. Prior to churches and the rise of monotheistic traditions, humans largely practiced forms of spirituality that were quite nature-based and animistic. In our wildest state, humans are deeply spiritual and look to nature with reverence and awe. We deeply connect with the possibilities of *something* beyond ourselves.

In contrast to the worldview of our ancestors, science seems to be the "church" of modern times. Additionally, our society seems to have placed a wedge between science and spirituality that really has no business being there. In the mainstream, spirituality is often even scoffed at as if it is something that belongs on the fringe. This is a major disservice to our animal nature, as each of us carries the primal desire for spiritual fulfillment. In rewilding ourselves and strengthening our ties to nature, we can tap into a very powerful form of feral self-care and honor the awestruck lil' tree goblin within!

There is something inherently spiritual in cultivating a relationship with not only nature but your *own* wild, the messy, uncivilized bits of you that tug at the fringes of your awareness. Indeed, the feral creature that lives inside of you is not one to be caged and kept at bay, but to be unleashed! This may be the way to satisfy that spiritual longing we feel when we stare at the ocean or gaze at the stars. That longing comes from a certainty that there is something more—something deliciously mysterious, both ever-present and elusive, that we can feel.

There is no religion in the endeavor of worshipping your wild—no rules to follow or churches to be seated in. The phrase "Your body is a temple" gains more meaning when you realize that through the sensory portal of your body you can taste something larger than yourself at the foot of the cosmos. By approaching your own rewilding and relationship with nature as a spiritual journey, we can move out of the realm of civilized logic and lean back into the primal frequency of being a *part* of the natural ecosystem rather than the dominator of it. This is a deeply restorative act of self-care.

How to Do It

To begin worshipping your wild, approach your relationship to nature as one of reverence. The relationship we forge with our earthly home can be both grounding, practical, and spiritual in nature. To foster this connection, take the time to interface with nature in whatever way feels best for you. Some examples:

- Taking up foraging.
- Swimming in the sea.
- Staring at the stars.
- Dancing in the rain.

Whatever you do, approach it from a place of awe and wonder. Any given human lifetime is so brief, and it is a beautiful thing to truly soak up all the natural beauty that there is in the world and to remember that if all the skyscrapers, cars, clothing, and *stuff* were to be gone, it would once again be nature that nourishes and cradles you.

Beyond this, every time you honor your natural instincts, move with intuition, allow your life to be a creative portal to fun and spontaneity, and follow your own authentically unhinged spirit, you are worshipping at the altar of your wild. So go forth, be connected, be free, and be fulfilled!

Watch the Skies

Long before there was TV and smartphones, people looked to the skies. Although the channel can't be changed, there's a lot going on up there at any given point that can both inform and delight. As human beings, the sky has played a huge role in our lives throughout history. People could (and still can) use the sky to predict weather, to gaze at the cosmos in wonder, and to guide cycles of waking and rest. As a creature of this planet, your life is deeply influenced by the sky, and no amount of technological progress can lessen its impact on you!

Although you may no longer be in the position to rely on the sky for things like predicting weather or finding your way while traveling, there is still a lot to be gained by taking the time to turn your attention skyward. The importance of doing this is felt intuitively when stargazing or watching a beautiful sunset. You may find it awakens a very primal part of you. As you look upward you can be humbled at just how much natural beauty exists and also reminded again that human problems are very small at the foot of nature. Complex and dynamic, the sky continues to be a source of fascination and wonder.

In self-care terms, skygazing can feel like a proper antidote to the busyness and constant technological connection that has become such a staple of modern life. There is a feral creature within you that's nourished by nature, and you can help satisfy that creature by watching storms, lazily picking out shapes in clouds, and just drinking it all in. To skygaze is to slow down and to face the larger cosmic system of nature that you exist in.

How to Do It

You can approach skygazing in many different ways, but the following are a few easy ways to get the most bang for your buck while being easy to fit into a hectic life:

- **Cloud watching:** Find a clear and safe area to lie down and look at the sky. As you lie there, allow your mind to wander. Pay attention to what comes up, but allow your mind to drift as it wants. Look at the shapes of the clouds and also their movement and pace. Make note of any images you see in them. The human brain is hardwired to spot symbols and recognizable structures (faces, animals) in ambiguous stimuli, so what is it you see? How do these things change as you're watching?
- **Stargazing:** A great time to do this in the Western Hemisphere is during the summer meteor showers. Look online for when these showers may be visible in your area. As you stare at the sky you may notice a lot going on up there. There are a lot of visible satellites in the modern sky, but try and imagine what it may have looked like for your ancestors prior to modern civilization.
- **Watching a sunrise or sunset:** One of the most primal truths in any human life is that life is fleeting. And in the modern era it's easy to drift into living on autopilot. Jump-start your system by breaking routine and taking the opportunity to intentionally go out and appreciate a sunrise or sunset. I personally find doing this on the solstices or equinoxes can be especially potent.

It is your birthright as an inhabitant of this planet to enjoy the sky. To give yourself the time and space to incorporate this into your day is a wonderfully simple form of feral self-care!

Bring Nature Indoors

As has already been established, getting down with nature can be a robust dimension of embracing your feral self—however, what do you do if you are living in an urban area without easy access? What if you aren't "outdoorsy" and a frolic in the woods would make you feel more tense than tapped in?

Even if you're a city slicker or a person with zero desire to stomp around outside, you can still get the benefits of nature by bringing a little of it indoors. The feral self-care that comes with aligning yourself to nature is not only reserved for those who gleefully immerse themselves in it. Many people can also benefit from taking nature in small doses by incorporating things like potted plants into their spaces and home decor.

There has been a lot of scientific research on the effects of nature on human wellness. One angle of this research has been concerned with houseplants—mainly, what effect keeping them has on your well-being. Unsurprisingly, the results show what you already feel deep in your ancestral DNA! Even the simple act of tending to houseplants in the home can have many benefits, including helping you be happier, less stressed, and enjoy better air quality in your living spaces.

In many houseplant groups online you can get a peek into the mental health benefits of plant keeping as well. For some, taking care of houseplants can provide a sense of purpose even in the darkest depths of depression. For others, plants are a source of low-maintenance companionship and joy. And on a primal level people have evolved to enjoy sticking their hands in the dirt, tending and caring for nature. You can satisfy that vital desire by bringing in some leafy roommates.

How to Do It

1. To begin the task of bringing nature into your space as a form of feral self-care, get yourself one potted plant. Although there is a definite learning curve to becoming a plant parent, there are some plants that are easier and lower maintenance than others, such as a snake plant or a pothos. That being said, your results may vary. I've had personal experience with killing a great many plants that always appear on those "easiest plant" listicles!

2. Once you have your plant, learn the conditions it needs to thrive, and commit yourself to its service. Touch the soil with your bare fingers, dust off its leaves, move it if it seems unhappy in its location. The thing about plant care is that it can often be a case of trial and error and an exercise in openness and patience. It certainly isn't the sort of thing that's worth beating yourself up over, as even a dead plant is representative of lessons learned and knowledge gained.

3. If you want to improve your chances of your plants surviving, get yourself a moisture meter. They're inexpensive and can help lower your kill rate by a long shot.

4. As you tend to your plants, make sure to make it a mindful and meaningful experience. As cheesy as it may sound, we humans are truly fortunate to get to share space with these organisms and to be able to incorporate them into our lives even in the most urban settings.

Observe Microworlds

Sometimes, in the midst of the daily grind, it can feel that these heavy human problems are all that there is. In the chaos of paying bills, trying to survive, and attempting to stay sane, it can feel as if the issues and problems we face are all consuming. However, when you get a chance to take a break and retreat into more natural settings, the brain fog lifts and you can once again be reminded that human problems are just that: *human* issues. There are many other layers of reality both large and small that aren't so engrossed in the bullshit of humanity.

When I was a small child, one of my favorite pastimes was searching for hidden microworlds in nature. These are the little fairy scenes that are incredibly small, yet somehow mimic the larger landscapes of the world. As the mystics would say: As above, so below. I would lose hours looking for these fairy worlds, imagining taller bits of moss as trees, blankets of lichen on rocks as the grass. When looking at these worlds up close, younger me would feel like a giant, peering in on a forest that was much, much smaller. The human struggles of being a small child in a very big world would melt away because at the foot of Mother Nature we are all small children. Not knowing much of anything at all and powerless to the larger complexities of the universe. When you begin to look so closely at these tiny ecosystems, it's a humbling experience, as you get valuable perspective that there is so much going on at every level, from the larger scale of the galaxy to the imperceptive microscopic plane.

As a form of feral self-care, the benefits of seeking out these microworlds come not only from the attention given to nature and the time spent rewilding but also by lazily interfacing with nature—finding pleasure from simply the act itself. A walk to search for these worlds is not a busy endeavor—no—it is one to mindfully and lazily soak up all the visual wonder and complexity of the natural world.

How to Do It

The next time you are on a hike or walk outdoors, slow way down and look carefully for little microworlds. They can be the patches of moss on boulders, the "fairy rings" or wide circles of mushrooms that sometimes spring up in the grass, or the blooming patches of lichen on the trees. Apart from being pleasing to the eye, these little worlds are a reminder that while human life has us busy rushing about from here to there in this modern world of chaos, nature is still radiating peace and stillness on both the macro- and microscale.

As you look at these tiny worlds, think about how skewed our perceptions are. To search for these microworlds is to gain an important new perspective: You too are very small in regard to the larger natural world, and your problems are not all-consuming. They are simply consuming *you*. There is so much going on in nature, and things continue to thrive regardless of whether rent is due or taxes are paid.

When looking at these microworlds, you can lean back into the feeling of childlike wonder and primal appreciation for nature. There is so much beauty and complexity right under your feet. Tap into feral self-care by taking the time to slow down and appreciate it!

Enjoy Some Natural ASMR

One thing about the modern world is that it is *loud*. It can feel as if there's an audio assault coming from all angles, with the sounds of vehicles, city construction, other humans, and a seemingly endless list of noises barreling into our ears and scrambling our brains. It can be almost unavoidable as well, as even if you drive out to the wilderness for a hike, the silence can be interrupted by the drone of airplanes overhead in the sky. Human beings are a nuisance when it comes to sound pollution (the constant background din of human activity), which can leave us yearning for silence and a break from the noise of modern life.

However, nature itself is also loud. Through day and night there's a regular symphony of sound in the form of bugs, animals, and sometimes deep, thunderous rumbles in the sky. However, this kind of noise hits the human ear differently. These are the noises that our species "grew up" with, and your human ears delight in the lilting tune of birdsong or in the rushing of water. This natural symphony, chaotic as it is, seems to have the opposite effect on well-being as human-made noise. While the cacophony of society can leave you feeling tense and overstimulated, the soothing sounds of nature act as music to your feral ears. The symphony of the natural world can sometimes be a better alternative to silence even and can unlock a primal source of contentment and peace.

Prior to civilization, these nature sounds were the soundtrack for life. There is something very primal inside you that is still soothed by hearing the orchestra of nature. Whether it be the sound of rolling thunder or the song of morning birds, you can find some feral self-care by reveling in the sounds of nature and allowing yourself to be fully and mindfully present in your body to enjoy them.

How to Do It

1. Venture out into nature where you can be undisturbed. For maximum impact if you are in the city, do this activity in the early mornings before the traffic and city noise begin to take over. If possible, try to do it in a more natural setting, such as on a nature hike or if you have access to somewhere rural. That being said, city parks can do the trick, provided you can find some time and space when it isn't busy or if your mental filter is good enough to tune out the rest of society.

2. Once you find a good place, get seated comfortably and just listen. What do you hear? Are there birds singing? Trees rustling? Squirrels chattering? Whatever it is, just sit with it and enjoy. Take note of how these sounds feel in your body, where you feel them, and how they affect you. Use mindful awareness to pay attention to the natural sounds around you, sinking into the power of your animal body to delight in these sensations. (Feel free to pair this activity with some deep breathing so that you can really maximize the chill zone.)

3. As you sit and take it all in, think about your feral ancestors and what it must have been like when this was the musical background of life. Let the uncivilized creature within you delight in the unruly yet soothing sounds of your neighbors on this planet.

Nourish Yourself with Plants

Here's a shower thought for you: Human beings once lived solely off of things that they found, foraged, and hunted. Prior to the age of the grocery chain, they had to look to what the earth gave them for food and medicines. Now, clearly, the modern age has benefited people a great deal in this way, as many are undoubtedly more well fed and more likely to survive medical and health issues than in early times. However, it is still a vital part of the human experience to look to plants for nourishment and healing.

Having plants as a large part of your diet and wellness regimen is something that is a fundamental part of the human experience. Although people are now cursed with the scourge of cheap and readily available, overly processed foods, plants were once the "mother's milk" for the human species. The species as a whole essentially "grew up" on plants that were used for food, medicine, personal care, and a variety of other issues. Because of this, human life is intertwined with the use of plants, and although life looks very different now, you can still benefit from incorporating more plants into your self-care routines.

Aside from just feeding you, plants have also been a huge part of humanity's quest for health and wellness. Ingestion and application of plants has had spiritual and medical significance for ages, particularly before the rise of pharmaceutical advances. Herbalism, using plants for healing and medicine, has been a part of human life for about as long as people have existed. For example, white willow bark used for pain relief and turmeric used for inflammation. This knowledge was the precursor to modern medicine, and although modern medicine has been a fortunate development, you can still benefit from incorporating the healing power of plants into your life (for example, drinking chamomile tea to help you relax).

So if you want to align yourself with the delicious wild that's hidden deep within you, nourish yourself with plants as an avenue to feral self-care!

How to Do It

There are a variety of ways to begin to incorporate more plants into your diet and wellness routines. For some, this might start with adding more fresh fruits and vegetables into their diet, while others may look toward herbalism for more medicinal uses. Whether it be the use of teas, foods, or seasonings, there are so many ways to feed yourself with plants. If you are interested in learning more about specifics, there is a wealth of reliable resources online, and there are many herbalism books available.

As part of this endeavor, you may want to use plants that you have a relationship with—for example, plants you have grown or foraged yourself. However, this isn't necessary and shouldn't be a barrier for those just starting out. You can still gain the benefits whether you get your plants from the farmers' market or grocery store.

It's important to note that if you are having any sort of medical issues, seeing a doctor is the best self-care strategy. This animal body you cart around has benefited a great deal from the incredible advances in technology and medicine in the modern era. There is no denying that! However, in many cases, your health and wellness would still benefit from getting more plants in, whether it be through your diet or as supplemental self-care in the form of teas, tinctures, and the like. Just remember to always consult with your doctor when adding new shit into your wellness regimen.

Dance in the Rain

One of the ways humanity has become more comfortable and successful has been due to our ability to sidestep the weather. While the weather was a hugely influential part of the everyday life and activities of your ancestors, modern human activity can more or less continue despite the onslaught from the sky. And many are fortunate enough to enjoy a significant amount of comfort regardless of what's happening outside. You can work, travel, collect food, and play in temperature-controlled conditions, well insulated from whatever Mother Nature is throwing at you.

As you've been learning throughout this chapter, humans carry a deep and primal instinct to align with the cycles of nature. And the weather is one expression of those cycles. Yes, you are undeniably better off to have the present-day comforts that keep you safe and protected from the most dangerous aspects of weather. However, you can also take the time to honor your animal nature by vibing in alignment with the weather.

As modern humans, we sometimes need to be jolted awake from the dangerous spell of living on autopilot. Feral self-care strategies like connecting to weather allow you to do that while also letting you activate the primal animal within! Your next feral self-care task is to get out there and enjoy the weather, not only when it's sunny and easy to do so, but in the full spectrum of what Mother Nature has to offer—the rain, the snow, and the storms!

How to Do It

Although there are many ways to frolic and delight in the many expressions of weather, dancing in the rain is a particularly wild one. Like most feral self-care, to dance in the rain might sound insane or like some romanticized movie scene, but in reality it can be a great way to shake off the apathy of modern-day life and jolt yourself into feeling awake and alive! Having access to a private yard works best for this; however, you can commit to this full expression of your authenticity anywhere. Basically, the method is exactly as it sounds: Go out when it's raining, dressed however you choose, and simply frolic and dance around. Do you feel completely unhinged? *Good!* This is the purpose of going feral when it comes to self-care. You are meant to awaken into the fullness of being alive, in this human body, on this stunning planet! Do this activity for as long or as little as you please, but take special notice of how it feels in your body and in your mind.

Alternatively, if you have a covered balcony or somewhere you can safely watch a storm, take the opportunity to do so! You can use LED candles, pop on some music, whatever you choose to make the activity even more fun. It is a fantastic form of feral self-care as you can feel the atmospheric electricity in the air through your body while also getting an amazing show.

Feel free to think of the specific weather in your region, and brainstorm other ways you can play in it! To go feral is to reconnect to your primal body and really revel in the experience of being a human on this planet. Playing in the weather is a vital part of that experience.

Play with the Seasons

Part of the reason why adult life feels as if it is passing us by at break-neck speed is because we aren't encouraged to take the time to truly *live*. For children, time is experienced slower, as they live with reckless wild abandon, collecting all sorts of exciting, novel experiences. With all the responsibilities and obligations we have as adults, we can get caught in this trap of being robbed of our own lives. It can be really hard to find the time and energy to just frolic in the *experience* of being a human. Add to this the weird social ideas of how grownups *should* behave, and you have the perfect recipe for folks to miss out on their lives.

Enough!

You can find feral self-care in allowing yourself the space and opportunities to go out and truly *be* wild. One part of reclaiming this wild is to align with the seasons. For your ancestors, the seasons once determined many aspects of life; however, now that many people live lives of convenience, this is often no longer the case. You are now able to be separated from what's going on outside. In the process you might be missing out on some top-tier feral self-care opportunities!

It is deeply restorative to approach the seasons in the spirit of play. Just as a young child would dive into leaf piles and play around in the snow, you can also as an adult take the opportunity to truly live wildly by playing with the seasons!

How to Do It

To get some feral self-care with the seasons, simply go out and do something that is seasonally specific. This will depend heavily on your access to outdoor spaces and the expression of seasons in your area. Obviously factor in safety—for example, skinny-dipping in below-freezing temperatures is not a great plan!

Here are ideas of some things you can do to play with the seasons:

- **Spring:** Look for budding plants, smell the grass after rain, splash around in the mud, twirl in the rain, put your bare feet in the grass, stand in the sun, go bug-watching, plant some things, forage for early-spring flowers and herbs.
- **Summer:** Lie in the sun, run on a beach, go skinny-dipping, forage for summer flowers and herbs, make a nature mandala out of rocks and leaves, frolic barefoot in the grass, wake up early and stay up late to greet/say goodbye to the sun on the solstice.
- **Fall:** Crunch leaves on a walk, dive into big piles of raked leaves, prepare your garden for winter, look for mushrooms, play in the rain, go for twilight walks, smell the scent of fall (when you know, you know), make art with fallen leaves.
- **Winter:** Build a snow fort, go sledding, stare at the stars when it gets dark earlier, take a frosty walk to admire nature gone dormant (followed by cups of hot tea), visit an icy lake and listen to the sounds of the water underneath, make a snow angel (yes, like kids do!).

Feel free to add your own ideas to this list if anything pops into your mind. As with most things feral self-care, the idea is to just go out and *live*, aligned with nature, wild and free with no regard to arbitrary social rules for how you *should* conduct yourself. What's the point of even being a grownup if you don't get the perks of not having to give a shit about things like that!?

Walk Around

While our ancestors once roamed the land in search of what they needed to survive, the modern era is characterized by a lot of time spent sitting on our asses. If this sounds pretty dire, apparently it is. Research says that a lack of physical activity, while pleasant in the short term, has a lot of detrimental effects on your body, mind, and, by extension, society at large. Humans, once a species of movers and shakers (albeit maybe not in the best of circumstances), are now an easily winded shadow of those who came before. Surely there has to be a middle ground?

Your animal body is meant to move. You have evolved to be active; your nomadic hunter-gatherer ancestors had many opportunities to walk and run, and these activities were hallmarks of primitive human life. Although there are still unquestionably active humans today, to be vigorously active isn't as much a part of daily survival or our success as a species.

The plain truth is that exercise is good and necessary for the health and well-being of your mammalian form. Even just short amounts of low-impact exercise, such as walking, can have a dramatic effect on your wellness. It can help you prevent or lessen the impact of serious illness and disease, helps strengthen muscle and bone, and can play a huge role in the mental health realm (such as improving sleep and helping you feel less stress). Movement truly is medicine when it comes to the ailments of a modern sedentary lifestyle.

Even if you know exercise is good for you, in the modern age it's something that's more or less held off in a separate corner of life rather than a part of life itself. While trips to the gym are still worthwhile, your primal body yearns to have physical activity and motion be a meaningful part of the fabric of your life—not just another thing to schedule in on the fringes of it.

So indulge your animal body by walking or running in nature. Get back to a place of motion that can be as fulfilling in a feral sense as it is in a physical one.

How to Do It

If you are a person who is very sedentary, the first step is to literally take the first step! Choose a time and location in nature that feels easy and accessible to you, and start by walking. Resist the urge to do too much too fast. Your purpose here is simple: You are simply trying to give that feral beast inside you a little more activity. Sometimes it can help to put a little space between yourself and what you are doing—think of it as taking your "human" for a walk!

If you are already an avid walker and are looking to increase the benefits, maybe start to incorporate some running. Hell, you can even have fun with it and pretend you're an early hominid outrunning a predator!

By pairing these simple activities with time spent in nature, you get the chance to "double up" on the feral self-care returns. Earlier on in this chapter, you explored activities such as foraging, which require time spent outdoors walking, so feel free to pair this task with a previous one!

No matter where you're starting from, keep in mind that you are literally designed to do this! Your animal body evolved to move, and these meat machines we pilot are incredibly capable. Even if it's hard to start with, remember that all self-care requires breaking through some barriers, whether they be mental, emotional, or physical.

CHAPTER 3

EMBRACING THE FELT EXPERIENCES OF THE BODY

Within your feral spirit, there is a sensory gremlin that revels in the enjoyment that comes from this human experience! Your animal body is a portal that allows you to experience the fullness of life in all its messy, sensory glory. However, the domestication of humans has led most people to override or ignore the impulses and experiences of their senses in favor of the mind, often to their detriment. To follow your impulse, chase sensation, and mindfully sink into how it truly *feels* to be alive, is to honor the primal nature of your physical body, reintegrating the wisdom and pleasure that can come from these sensual urges.

In this chapter, you will connect with ways to get out of your head and back into your body by using easy somatic strategies and honoring your own sensory urges. It's time to go forth and feel it all—the sticky, soft, loud, rhythmic, savory, salty, colorful, shadowy experiences of your life! In the following practices, you will get to simultaneously experience and *create* these felt opportunities for revitalizing, joyful self-care.

Primally Scream

Despite rarely making those precious online wellness listicles of self-care ideas, I defy anyone to find a more satisfying way to blow off some steam and feel refreshed than a good old-fashioned primal scream! It truly is like a spa day for your feels.

In polite modern society, there's a resistance to saying how you *really* feel. A resistance that seems to increase in intensity when it comes to saying those things in an emotive way. Despite all the progress made in more recent years with encouraging folks to be themselves, talk about their feelings, and *blah blah blah,* the truth is that honest and unhinged emotional expression still seems to be uncomfortable for most—whether it be the doing *or* the witnessing.

However, to let out a primal scream is to engage in a practice that is very aligned to your natural animal instincts. It's the howling impulse that doubles as a release valve. It's simple, costs nothing, and doesn't require the participation of anybody else. With only your personal demons as witness, you can unhinge that jaw and let all the frustration, anger, and bad vibes flow out!

Screaming is passionate, a little taboo, and scratches a very serious itch most people have to *just let loose.* As a human being, you've likely experienced the pain of holding a big, explosive bitchbag of feelings. Anger, hurt, disappointment—these complex emotions can aggregate and churn within you, a discomfort that only gets worse the more you try and stuff it down or pretend it isn't there. What primal screaming allows you to do is to reclaim control of your body. Evicting all that dense, mucky energy through the power of emotive sound and vibration, lessening its power to tie your insides in knots.

Just let it all out, baby!

How to Do It

Now, you may be wondering how to get a scream in when the modern world is so insufferably *not* scream friendly. Society just isn't set up for you to primal scream on the spot in most contexts without all sorts of obnoxious, meddling interference. Luckily there are options that are as private as they are cathartic!

Self-Care Screamtivities That (Probably) Won't Result in a Wellness Check from the Police:

- Screaming into a pillow.
- Screaming in your car, alone.
- Screaming into your furniture (couches, mattresses).
- Screaming into the comfort of your blankets.
- Screaming during something fun where screaming is encouraged (e.g., on the roller coaster or at the haunted house).
- Screaming along to industrial/death metal music.
- [Your own ideas here!]

Now, many people have been conditioned since the earliest days of childhood to shush up and put a lid on authentic expression—particularly in the cases where doing so can make *others* uneasy. For this reason, it may take a little practice to get to a space where the screams flow freely. But try it and see how you feel. In most cases, primal screaming can lead to feeling lighter, happier (thanks to the rush of feel-good endorphins), and refreshed. The key is to muster up all that inner turmoil, providing it a channel for sweet release.

So if you have some stuff pent up that you need to exorcize, then give yourself a little scream as a treat! Your untamed nature deserves it!

Recklessly Embrace Pleasure

Sometimes self-care is about acknowledging pleasure and the unique role it plays in your experience of life. As has been said many times within these pages, you are a *mammal*. An animal! You have *needs*, dammit! And apart from the basic survival needs, humans also deeply crave the juicy and exciting pleasures of life. But along with our domestication, we've dropped truly owning these needs in favor of some uptight, self-denying bullshit. Especially when it comes to pleasure and allowing ourselves to simply enjoy things. Just for the sake of it.

Enough already!

In modern polite society, it often feels like when there is *anything* that feels good in life, it is banned as taboo. People then try to fake that they don't want that thing or put on this performance of holding themselves back from it because it's not "good" for them. You may do this with everything from sex to cookies. If it feels good just for the sake of feeling good, all of a sudden you may feel tempted to begin clutching your pearls and second-guessing your desires. In feral self-care terms, you can leave a lot on the table in regard to fulfillment and being kind to yourself when it comes to experiencing pleasure.

Allow me to clear my throat and shout that *not all pleasure is an opportunity for scandal!*

Look, you're allowed to *want* to be covered from head to toe in kisses. You're allowed to enjoy the cheesecake guilt-free sometimes. You're more than welcome to be a desire-fueled little gremlin. Just own it, enjoy it, and ditch the guilt already! It's no wonder you're so in need of self-care when you deny yourself so much. There is a feral creature inside you that wants to just be allowed to seek pleasure without the guilt, shame, and baggage.

Human beings evolved to feel pleasure, and it is a blessing. This human existence covers a wide range of experiences, from pleasure to pain. Your body is a portal that allows you to experience the fullness of life, and pleasure is a deep part of that—a part that is fulfilling and restorative. And this hits different when you allow yourself the privilege rather than holding yourself in a perpetual state of denial. To put it simply, pleasure and guilt do not have to be synonymous.

So lean into pleasure as a form of feral self-care. Allow yourself to delight in the indulgence of your sensual nature!

How to Do It

Drape yourself in silken robes, lie out on a cashmere rug, or indulge in your favorite treat just because it feels good. Run in that field (just watch out for ticks)! Eat that ice cream monstrosity! Lust after your spouse! Whatever feels good for you, *do that*. Right now. Do it unashamedly. Own it! Your physical body is a portal!

Lord knows, people have enough garbage to feel bad about in the modern age, so please, for the love of grass and all that is holy: Recognize that pleasure is one of the simplest joys that you can give yourself. This makes it a truly magical addition to your self-care tool kit. Indulge your animal nature and sink into the glorious physical and mental health benefits to follow.

Your assignment today is to do something that *feels* good. Period.

Do a Goblin Body Shake

Movement is medicine, and I'm not talking about phoning it in on a StairMaster at the gym. I mean finding some way to shake that thang in a way that feels *fun* and high vibe for you. Taking care of your physical body is a deeply important part of self-care, but when it comes to the medicine of movement, energies play a role as well. Moving your physical body also has the power to migrate stale energies in your energetic body, which can be keenly felt when you have a good dance session, run your heart out, or have a particularly satisfying stretch.

Although many people don't necessarily enjoy exercise in a formal, structured way, chances are you *might* enjoy other forms of vigorous movement, such as dancing like a maniac in your kitchen or something similar. Dancing and movement have been a primal form of expression for humans throughout history. Deep down inside, everyone is just an unhinged lil' primate seeking joy and release through the channel of their physical form. Indeed, having a body comes with the usual physical woes, but so too does it come with infinite opportunities for pleasure and play. Indulge in all that feral deliciousness!

It's important to note that this isn't exclusive for athletic or able-bodied folks either. Medicinal movement can be swaying your torso to a fun song, waving your arms, or simply giving a good ol' neck bob. There is *zero* judgment or expectations for a task like this. The *only* requirement is that you use your body as a vehicle for joy in whichever way you feel fit and reap the rewards that are bound to follow. It's time to move simply for the sake of catching a vibe!

How to Do It

So if you're wanting to think outside the box and indulge in a little feral self-care, get that booty moving and shaking! There's a reason the saying "Dance like nobody's watching" is so popular and enduring. Let loose and allow your body to be a vehicle for invigoratingly unhinged mammalian movement. You do not have to be a dancer, or athletic, or coordinated *at all*. The self-care benefits of a task like this aren't found in the performance, but in the *experience*.

Dance like the degenerate critter you are in order to call in more fun, happiness, and to get that energy flowing. Shake it, pop it, drop it low—anything goes! Just get that body and energy moving. Even if you might look silly. *Especially* if you might look silly. The fear of "doing it wrong" or looking unseemly is just the kind of domesticated bullshit you need to strip away and avoid. Your body is a portal for unhinged expression and joy without having to curate and hone your movement for others.

Set your spirit alight through the power of unhinged somatic whirling and prancing right now!

Find a Sunbeam, Become a Puddle

In the hustle and bustle of modern capitalist culture, there is neither time nor the gentle encouragement to just slow down, relax, and immerse yourself into your own life! Sadly, many people run on autopilot, rushing from place to place, responsibility to responsibility, without having the resources left over at the end of the day to take care of their own well-being.

The truth is that you are not meant to just have a sad little time block at the end of the day to cram in your wellness. You are meant to fully experience life, soaking it all up and finding purpose and growth along the way. This is why it's so important to take any and every little opportunity to follow your instincts and become mindfully present to the felt experience of your life. This includes rest. To rest is to not only give yourself space to pause but also allow yourself to actually enjoy the feelings of existing in your body, in living your life.

A powerful act of feral self-care is to find a sunbeam and simply laze around in it. There is something deeply and primally nourishing about soaking up the warm rays of the sun while lying in a feline-like heap on the floor. Is this a conventional act of self-care in modern polite society? Perhaps not. However, there are no rules on how to human, especially when trying to satisfy your animal instincts!

This act of feral self-care tasks you to slow down and connect with the portal of your body. It is a felt experience, one that simply jumps on the opportunity to sink into a moment of time with no expectations or rules to follow. This doesn't have to be your new routine or something to fit into your day. It just...is! Give yourself the permission to rest, laze around, and enjoy the pleasant sensations of your human form.

How to Do It

On a sunny day when you are home and the circumstances align just right for the chance to laze around in a sunbeam, drop what you're doing and *take it*:

1. Lie down on the floor in the light, even if it's just a slice. Find a position where you'll be able to feel the warmth and light.
2. Try and ensure that you are comfortable; you can use pillows or blankets to help cushion the experience.
3. Next, take some deep breaths and allow yourself to truly relax. Try to ignore any panicked impulses to get up and do something productive. Instead just lie there and try to be as present as possible, soaking up every moment. Your only job is to soak in the warm glow of that big, bright, radioactive siren in the sky.

Although it may seem like an unusual thing to do at first, just try it out and see how it feels. You might find yourself surprised by how good it feels to chase an impulse such as this, with little regard for conventional ideas of what modern-day self-care "should" look like!

Do a Self-Massage

As human beings, one of our most primal desires is for touch. We thrive on it and crave the feeling of being stroked, patted, rubbed, and massaged! Although this may sound kind of sexy-naughty or sensual, it doesn't have to be. Our need for touch goes deeper than just being something sexual in nature.

Even when you are touch starved, you have the ability to give that touch to yourself. And as a human being who has a sensory awareness of what's going on inside your body (such as aches, pains, itches, and the like), sometimes you are the best person to give yourself that touch! For example, engaging in self-massage can be a very powerful form of feral body care, as it can help you really become present in your physical body while also helping to relieve pain and discomfort that may be making you feel like shit. It can also be a really great way to just give your body a little love and attention without necessarily being a solution to any particular problem.

Giving yourself a massage is not only good for your wellness, promoting relaxation and reducing physical discomfort, but is also a tangible act of self-love. The animal body yearns for touch, and the sensation of massage in your body is a pleasant one. While it can be wonderful to go get a professional massage, for many people there are barriers to this (time, finances, etc.). By approaching massage as a DIY endeavor, you give yourself the gift of showing appreciation for your body while taking your self-care into your own hands (literally).

In Ayurveda, an alternative ancient Indian medicine system, there is something called *abhyanga*, which is the act of giving yourself a massage using oils. Although this is done to help the physical body in a practical sense, it is also approached in the spirit of love and thought to restore balance to a person's well-being. For those with body image issues, the gift of self-touch or self-massage in the spirit of love and care can be an act of radical self-acceptance. Part of feral self-care is understanding that the creature you are is always good and worthy, and that you in your most authentic and uncultivated state deserve all the love and care in the world.

How to Do It

1. Before you begin the process of self-massage, take a moment to set aside any judgment and to tell your inner critic to piss off. If you struggle with body image issues, perhaps take a *few* moments to do this. Remind yourself of the purpose at hand: giving your mammalian self some much-needed, well-deserved TLC!
2. Next, make sure your space is comfortable by choosing whatever lighting, sounds, and scents are soothing and relaxing for you.
3. Begin by focusing on one body part at a time and massaging with whatever pace and pressure helps to soothe or relieve your muscles.
4. As you massage, try to be present for the felt sensation of it. Tell yourself loving affirmations. Remind yourself how cool it is to be able to feel your life! Hunker down in the feeling of being a physical creature with a physical body. Massage only certain trouble spots, or proceed to work all your body if that feels right.

While this is an amazing and easily doable act of feral self-care, it's important to note that you should be cautious if you have any acute musculoskeletal issues that you could potentially trigger or make worse. Even in the spirit of uncivilized, primal felt experience, caution is key! Check in with your doctor about any concerns.

Co-Regulate with Creatures

Human beings did not evolve on this planet alone; they are but one species in a larger network and ecosystem of critters, both big and small. In many ways the relationship to these other creatures helped to shape and mold human evolution. These relationships have a history going back for many thousands of years.

Human beings have benefited from relationships with other species in a variety of ways. From our relations with agriculture animals, such as cows, to companionship animals, like dogs, the lives of humans have been influenced not in a small way by the role of animals. Even in polite modern society, it is probably considered more mainstream to have an animal live in your home than it is to walk around your neighborhood barefoot!

In the case of pet ownership, probably one of the most relatable examples of the human-animal connection in modern society, the relationship is largely mutually beneficial. The animal (whether it be a cat, dog, or something else) gets love, food, attention, and safety from the wild. However, you also get a hell of a lot: love, a sense of purpose, and possibly protection. Studies have even shown that having a pet can help in a very concrete physical way as well, with various physical and mental health benefits, such as reduced levels of anxiety and depression.

Co-regulation is a term for a calming connection that can happen between two creatures. While people typically use this term in the context of human-to-human relationships, it also is a fundamental part of pet ownership. Certainly in the case of dogs, for example, both the mammalian human and the pet co-regulate, calming each other down and finding a shared sense of peace and loving safety. Interspecies creature comfort!

Sometimes self-care is getting that wellness "assist" from another. This next feral self-care activity is not one that can be tackled alone. You are to give yourself the opportunity to find creature comfort in the presence of an animal.

How to Do It

1. If you have access to a safe and familiar animal, such as a pet (or the pet of a friend or family member), simply begin by approaching them with love and openness. Animals are far more in touch with their instinctive nature than most modern humans, and they can essentially "read" your energy.

2. As you interact with this animal, allow your worries and stresses to melt away. Allow yourself to enjoy and delight in the presence of this other creature. If it is an animal that likes being petted, take some enjoyment in the felt experience of this and of fostering this connection.

3. If this is your own pet and you have a good relationship, the next time you're feeling off-kilter, give your pet a nice cuddle. Take that opportunity for loving co-regulation. If your pet is not the "cuddlable" type, then simply sit near them and observe them with an open heart.

4. As you do this activity, imagine all the stresses and worries melting away, and enjoy the primal sensation of this intimate and healing source of creature comfort.

Get Messy with Food

When aligning to feral, there is a deep, gremlin-like urge to shuck off all the polite niceties of being a human being in the twenty-first century. The wild urge to sniff at dirt, collect hordes of shiny rocks, to roll about in the grass, and to eat giant bites of food straight out of our hands. Indeed, cutlery is a very subtle symbol of polite Western civilization. This is why "finger food" is so fun; it allows us to drop the restrictive cutlery culture and really just have at 'er!

This isn't to say you should go to that fancy dinner at your boss's house and begin slurping peas out of your palms, but it is to say that sometimes when you're in your own home, deep in your feels, whether or not you decide to forgo the plate and fork is truly only your own business. This is truly between you and your own demons, bless 'em!

There is something fun and kind of unhinged about eating from your hands like a sneaky goblin or medieval king. Clearly this depends on the food (for example, the difference between eating a muffin versus a regular slice of cake with your bare hands), but to break such an ingrained social norm in this way can be a surprising source of fun and indulgent feral self-care. A silly, unhinged way to say fuck domestication and the forks that come with it!

Life can be challenging and catapult us deep in our feelings sometimes. From a feral self-care perspective, the best way to cope with the bullshit is to just follow your impulses and break the rules of what we're "supposed" to be doing. When we lack the energy to cope in times of stress or trouble, dropping some of the pressure to act civilized and proper can free up energy to rejuvenate our spirits.

It's okay to act a little slobby sometimes!

In many cases, it can bring a lot of joy and perspective to just let loose and find self-care in acting a little unhinged and wild. Like a little break from reality, as a treat!

How to Do It

So the next time you're hungry and feeling some thangs, duck the forks and knives and eat something with your bare hands! Arrange yourself a little plate of finger foods and be mindfully present in your physical body as you eat it. Lean into the physical sensations and how it feels to do such a thing. Chances are you will simply enjoy the opportunity to stay still for a mindful meal, *or* in the cases when you may choose something less than socially thumbs-up (hello, brick of cheese), you may feel so unhinged and demented that at the very least you'll have a laugh. The important thing is to recognize that life is not all that serious as we've made it out to be. After all, society is an illusion, forks and knives are simply props.

Get messy and break the "rules" with food to assert dominance over the things that keep you tame! It's completely unnecessary and totally unhinged—which in feral terms makes it a valuable tool for self-care!

Let Your Inner Child Free

Inner child healing is not just for spiritual baddies and those in therapy. In truth, every person has an inner child that didn't cease to exist just because they got drop-kicked into adulthood. In many cases, this inner child might be kicking and screaming for compassion, love, and the space to play amidst the pesky responsibilities and obligations of adulthood!

When people are young, they are encouraged to play, have fun, and explore. Yet once they grow up, they are thrust into a world that feels hard and full of responsibilities. In the grown-up realm, time and energy is difficult to come by, leaving a joy-sized hole that was once filled with creative adventure. What's more, adults in modern society are not encouraged to play as they did as children—a damned shame when you consider just how badly every adult could use some fun!

Children are especially connected to their feral selves. Prior to picking up social conditioning, they truly do live wildly, aligned with the very natural human impulses everyone has to express themselves, have fun, and engage in imaginative play. Children do all of this with very little regard for what's polite or civilized. They simply just...live. Their dedication to chasing impulses and living in each moment is a shining example of the chaotic joy and powerful zest for life that is available to everyone who wishes to become untamed!

So if you want some feral self-care that is playful, healing, and powerful all at once, let your inner child loose! You are meant to have fun, play, and experience the sensory whirlwind of this life. Life must be *lived*, so no more prioritizing behaving in a civilized manner and holding yourself back from going out and living each day with enthusiasm and reckless, unhinged joy!

How to Do It

Think back to something you really loved to do as a child, then literally just do some of that (within reason, let's not put out an aging back or stress an injury). Perhaps this is finger painting, going on the swings, or splashing around in a lake. Some additional ideas:

- Coloring in a coloring book.
- Doing a paint-by-number kit.
- Making bath paints to scribble affirmations and doodle in your tub.
- Frolicking in a sprinkler.
- Going sledding.
- Making mud pies.

There are so many ways you can lean into play and childlike wonder in your life. Genuinely, if more people chose to do this, people would probably have a lot more fun as society as a whole. One of the most perplexing things about adulthood is that many seem to act the way they *think they should* beside a bunch of other people merely doing the same!

So find at least *one* thing to do per day to indulge your inner child or to shift into the untamed energy of childhood. Approach this task without self-consciousness or rules. Truly allow yourself to be free— think flailing limbs, dizzy spins, and behaving in a way that is downright uncivilized!

Feel Your Way Through Overwhelm

Although modern life is arguably safer and easier than it was for your hominid ancestors, the human species is plagued with soaring rates of depression and anxiety. It almost seems as if the easier life has become in survival terms, the harder it becomes for people to cope.

As a person who has struggled my entire life with debilitating anxiety and treatment-resistant depression, I'm intimately familiar with the feeling of a lack of safety in my own skull. In my experience, dealing with anxiety (or stress, or fear, or overwhelm) feels like becoming completely untethered. The emotion can feel like a spiral or "vortex" that pulls awareness up into a cloud of disembodied chaos above my head.

If this sounds familiar, the solution, as counterintuitive as it may seem, is to wrestle your awareness out of that vortex and back into your body. You may resist doing this because that is where you're feeling all of the anxiety-induced alarm bells going off. But if you let yourself sit with it for a moment, it's like jumping into a body of water for a swim. Your physical body takes the shock, then slowly begins to acclimate, and you are then able to integrate and cope with whatever you are faced with.

As a sensory portal, your animal body delights in the many varied sensations of life. You get to experience it all—the sticky, prickly, soft, squishy, smooth textures of life. And they all affect you differently at different times. This is something that you can use to your benefit when trying to become grounded during feelings of overwhelm. By using tactile strategies, the felt sensation and perception of touch, you can begin to feel more grounded in your body and sink mindfully into a state of primal felt awareness.

No matter what it is you're dealing with, on a primal level you are alive. You are able to breathe and feel, and sometimes that's all that's required to help you cope in each given moment.

How to Do It

Your feral self-care task is simple: The next time you're feeling overwhelmed or you get sucked into that vortex, engage in something tactile as a way to reground your body and calm your nervous system.

When you're feeling stressed, overwhelmed, like you want to shuck off your skin suit and crawl into a hole, grab a stress ball, raid your kids' playdough stash, or run your hands over some textured fabric that's a sensory "fuck yes." Try to not focus on the unhinged, disembodied screaming of the brain but on the tactile experience you are having. For best results, pair this with intentional breathing, or hell, even a primal scream!

Sometimes the best act of feral self-care is to simply allow yourself to be present in your body. Your problems and worries are always going to be there ready to knock you off-kilter, so it's better to make your body a more stable and safe-feeling space to be.

Speak Out Loud to Yourself

Although humans evolved in community, and social relationships are an incredibly important part of a meaningful life, it is the relationship you have with yourself that can make or break you.

Certainly in modern culture it can be difficult not to slip into a trap of self-comparisons and grief about all the things that potentially may suck about ourselves and our lives. To some degree, feeling lost and insecure has been normalized, and many wind up internalizing these ideas that they aren't enough.

Although you can talk to other people about these feelings, at the end of the day when you are alone, who is going to calm and comfort you?

You need to be speaking to—and supporting—yourself.

In civilized society, talking to yourself is a little...out of the ordinary. However, it can actually be an especially potent act of self-care! Words are spells, and in many cases the things we tell ourselves about who we are become part of our personal lore and experienced reality. Although affirmations are often dismissed as cheesy, we do know that through affirmations and better self-talk, we become more confident and accepting of ourselves rather than letting our fears and insecurities run the show. When we become mindful of the messages we are giving ourselves, we begin the process of becoming our own best ally rather than endlessly shit-talking ourselves.

Additionally, there are different parts of the brain that formulate language, speak it, and hear it. When approaching the process of speaking kindly to yourself, why not do it out loud so that your brain has the chance to process these thoughts and messages in a few different ways?

Everyone needs support and love, and not only when feeling social. Your next feral self-care task is to adopt the somewhat unconventional habit of talking to yourself.

How to Do It

The next time you're alone and trying to sort out a problem or are plagued with anxiety or stress, initiate a conversation with yourself out loud. Remember, feral self-care is throwing out polite notions of how you "should" behave in favor of doing things that actually serve you. Although you might feel a bit silly to begin with, remind yourself that there are no witnesses here and nobody to judge you. It's just you and your demons, baby! Here are easy steps to follow:

1. When you are ready to try it, start talking out loud about how you feel and why. Research says that in doing this, you can help yourself process better. So get it all out; let it all flow!
2. Next, think of anything that could be said to alleviate your troubles, and say it out loud to yourself as if you were a loving third party. If it helps to do so, saying it in front of a mirror can help boost the self-care benefits. You can also bring your affirmations, words of encouragement, and expressions of gratitude to the mirror to boost this practice.

At the end of the day, you must be your own biggest ally. There's a whole big, wide world out there just teeming with messages about how you aren't enough as you are and pushing various reasons to feel "lesser than" upon you. At least when you're alone, you should get a reprieve from the madness and begin to cultivate a relationship where you can be your own little quirky best friend.

Indulge In Sexual Healing

There are many ways that humans have disconnected from our true animal nature in the modern world, but you can see this especially in the case of sex. With all the pearl clutching about this topic, you'd almost believe that sexual desire was some sort of defect rather than a fundamental aspect of the human experience. Despite any prudish notions and internalized hang-ups that surround the topic of sex, it is *literally* the thing that keeps the human species going. You are a sexual being; it is a foundational part of your animal nature to have desire, sensual urges, and the ability to find pleasure in that.

If you're wanting to add some sexual healing into your feral self-care strategy, take up the task of approaching sexuality without guilt or shame. Embracing your sexuality doesn't necessarily mean intercourse or orgasms either. It's bigger than that. In mental/energetic terms it's about accepting the sexual dimension of this human experience without fear or feeling "bad." It's about trading in self-denial for curiosity and play. It's about accepting that aspect of your mammalian self without all the typical hang-ups that pop up when factoring in how society expects people to look, behave, or approach this dimension of themselves. In a physical sense, it's about embracing the portal of your body specifically when it comes to pleasure. Are you accepting of your body? Or does it interfere with your ability to let go in the moment?

Letting go is the key for sexual healing. Modern society has made this entire topic so wrapped up in taboo that many end up trying to deny this aspect of themselves or approach it with guilt or shame.

You can be both a feral gremlin *and* a sexual creature! Your approach to sexuality is fully your own and isn't reliant on fitting in any sort of box. So let's take this conversation out of the fringes of polite domestication and make peace with the fact that this is a fundamental dimension of the human experience. One that you can approach safely and openly, and one that doesn't require you to look or act in a certain way to be "doing it right."

How to Do It

One way to approach embracing your sexuality is to find what makes you feel sexy. Maybe it's a certain outfit or activity, such as dancing. Maybe it's allowing yourself to fantasize freely without letting guilt and shame mess with your flow. Whatever it is, embrace it and see how you feel when you do so with openness in the spirit of letting go.

Another crucial element for embracing your sexuality is to approach it in the primal sense. Recognize that this is a foundational need of being a human mammal. Much like eating or breathing. Treat it as such!

Whether it be with a partner or by yourself, it's important to approach this feral self-care concept with an open mind and an open heart. Many people carry sexual traumas and hang-ups that don't need to undermine their approach to sexuality forever. Therapy can be helpful in cases of trauma, and it's important to examine your hang-ups to figure out how much of these are just conditioned ideas that have been absorbed by living in a society that's always telling you that you fall short.

Eat for Pleasure

Despite the fact that people now have a million things they feel they have to do to be successful in life, at a primal level there are just a few: eating, drinking, sleeping. While your creature body needs nourishment, in present life eating has become somewhat complicated. With the easy availability of overly processed dopamine-boosting food and society seeming to revolve around lofty and unrealistic beauty ideals, this simple function of human survival has become fraught with guilt, shame, and other complicated feelings. Diet culture, the idea that you should eat and look a certain way or be a certain size or shape in order to be "good" or "acceptable," has got people fucked up when it comes to food.

Part of going feral is enjoying the sensory dimension of life—the novel experiences and pleasures you can access through your body. Eating is a part of this. Eating is not simply beneficial in terms of survival but can actually be a *pleasurable* experience! Your body is a miracle that can not only be nourished but also gain pleasure from that nourishment. While it's true that the foods you have readily available to you in most modern settings are not necessarily the most supportive to your health and well-being, it can be dangerous to ascribe to moral codes for food. The real question isn't whether the food is "good" or "bad" but whether it is in alignment with how you want to nourish yourself and how you want to feel.

There is something very healing about allowing yourself to find pleasure in food. When you strip away the modern context, whether it be the types of food that are common or the attitudes toward them, you're left with the human creature that can (and should!) have the joy of being able to experience a vital kind of pleasure through food.

How to Do It

Treat yourself as a way to gain some feral self-care through food! Give yourself the gift of nonjudgmentally allowing yourself the experience of pleasure through food. If you have struggled with food issues or comfortably allowing yourself to find enjoyment in food, this might be a more challenging task; however, the benefit of trying it may be greater!

1. To begin, reflect on the biology of human nourishment. That you are an animal that needs food, but that you are also an animal that gets to *enjoy* food.
2. Next, choose something delicious that you like to eat. To lean into the energy of going feral, perhaps you could bake yourself something or indulge in foods from nature that will delight your primal senses (fruit is fantastic for this). Many people go for something sweet, a treat that will delight and tickle the taste buds. No matter what you choose, make sure it is something that will provide a sensorily pleasurable experience.
3. Next, sit down and indulge in that food with the goal to savor every moment of it completely guilt-free. This is a gift from you to you! Allow yourself to enjoy not only the taste but the very pleasure of eating.

Nourish Your Face

When you close your eyes and envision your most feral self, you may see a hairy swamp goblin, frolicking in mud and absolutely *loving* it. However, your human form doesn't need to match that aesthetic. As feral as you are, you likely feel the desire to feel pampered and beautiful sometimes, which is why the stereotypical "spa day" is like the unofficial mascot of beauty self-care. But what's a feral creature to do when they're short on time or coins to make this happen?

Luckily, you live in a world full of gifts from nature! It's important that you stop and remind yourself that human beings did just fine for ages long before TV screens were throwing their biggest flaws back at them in every commercial. Humans existed long before any of that shit. Your ancestors used to forage and craft all sorts of remedies, medicines, and primitive products that were all natural and served their purposes. This isn't to say that you shouldn't indulge in things that are manufactured—just that there are other opportunities available to you. Even things as simple as basic foods could be used for a variety of things, and you can benefit from some of this DIY energy when it comes to your beauty care. After all, what's more unhinged than slathering food on your face?

DIY edible beauty care products can be a totally fun way to both take care of your body and feel totally unhinged. By going this route, you can make your own natural concoctions that won't contain all the extra unpronounceable ingredients or come with the high price tag. Additionally, you might find yourself feeling refreshingly uncivilized.

Lean into the feral self-care ethos by working with what you have on hand, especially if it serves dual purposes. It's beauty self-care meets goblin mode!

How to Do It

There are many foods that are safe and even beneficial to use on your face. Pick a fun food that suits what you're needing, then smash it up and smear it on your face for a natural face mask!

Some common household foods that work well in face masks are:

- **Honey:** Honey (specifically raw honey) has been used by humans for beauty care for ages. It can be helpful for treating acne, reducing inflammation, and brightening the look of the skin.
- **Oatmeal:** Oatmeal is a fantastic remedy for itching and can help hydrate and soften skin. It can also help to soothe and reduce redness if you're having skin issues.
- **Banana:** Bananas are full of vitamins and other good nutrients that can nourish and strengthen your skin.
- **Avocado:** Avocados are great to smash on your face to make your skin softer and more hydrated. Like bananas, avocados are also full of a lot of nourishing things for your skin.

Now it should go without saying, but make sure and test each of these on your skin prior to slathering it on. Every body is different, and even if you are able to eat these foods, it doesn't mean you aren't at risk for having a dermal reaction. Going feral doesn't need to come with an unintended rash!

Take a Mindful Bite

As you've read about a million times in these pages, your body is a portal! To take for granted the sensory opportunities available to you through the body is to go through life without fully *experiencing* it. Unfortunately, this is what all too many people do in modern life. It's far too easy to spend so much time rushing around in the realm of frivolous human affairs that you find yourself running on autopilot, missing the experiences that come with being fully, dizzyingly alive!

Fundamentally, eating is a primal necessity and (obviously) a pretty big priority. You *need* to do this to live. However, unlike a house pet who receives the same meal of kibble every day, you are able to experience additional sensations to fullness or hunger. Things like pleasure, disgust, and satisfaction to name a few. Eating can be a very basic form of both nourishment and sensory experience. There is a huge difference between nourishing yourself by scarfing down a sandwich in the car or eating trail mix over your desk and the intentional act of mindful eating.

Mindful eating is when you take the time to slow down and become fully present for the experience of feeding yourself. One of the perks of this human experience is that your body can take you to some delicious sensory places. *Let it!* Life is so busy and full of chaos and chatter that to slow down and be fully present for something as simple and necessary as eating can be an immensely rewarding form of self-care. After all, self-care is not just pampering yourself: It is taking care of your wellness as a whole. As a primal creature, you can get these benefits in both body and mind.

How to Do It

For this feral self-care task, your assignment is to simply slow down! Choose a meal when you have the time and attention to spare, and try to set it up as a full experience. This can include setting up your table fully and creating a mood with lights and music before digging in. Or it may include sitting on the couch naked eating leftovers at 2 a.m. The food itself is not the focus; it is the act and experience of eating that is!

That being said, it is not just the eating that can be part of the experience. You can bring the energy of mindfulness to choosing and preparing your food, whether it be grocery shopped, foraged, or cooked on your own! You can also pay attention to how the food you eat makes you feel, another benefit of slowing down and listening to your body.

So if you want to tackle some feral self-care that is not just physical but experiential as well, try mindful eating. Approach your meals as an opportunity to have a primal felt experience beyond nourishment, and see how it feels!

Connect to Your Breath

A very important aspect of this human experience that people tend to take for granted is breathing itself. The simple act of taking in oxygen is one of your most important jobs. Indeed, paying bills, doing a good job at work, etc.—all of this comes secondary to the fundamental task to just simply breathe! While to breathe is automatic, to breathe intentionally can be a game changer!

Overwhelm is a looming presence in everyday human life, and returning to the breath can be a simple but powerful form of self-care. Many times when you are in a state of busyness or stress, your breath pattern is naturally interrupted. As you tense up, you may pause your breath. As you spiral, you may begin to hyperventilate, resulting in a shallow and rapid breath pattern. In both of these cases, your ability to deal with what you're faced with is fundamentally impaired, as your breathing can rile you up or calm you down.

In the tooth-grinding, tense-shoulder hustle and bustle of life in this society, to slow down and take control of your breath is to begin to take control of yourself. Anxiety, stress, and overwhelm cannot be "cured" in all cases with breathing; however, if you slow down and take note of your breath, you may put enough space between yourself and those feelings of chaos that you are more able to cope in a grounded and functional way. In the intentional act of taking in breath, you are able to give your brain and body a leg up on the pressure rather than have your animal body spiral even more into crisis.

So if you're looking for a little self-care that is free, easy, and feeds into the well-being of your primal animal body, then take a minute to return to your breath.

How to Do It

1. To begin, take notice of what your breath is naturally doing in one of those moments when you're feeling overwhelmed by fuckery and wanting to crawl out of your own skin. Are you tense and accidentally holding your breath? Are you breathing in a way that is rapid and shallow? Try to block out other sensations and pay keen attention to what is happening in your body and your lungs.

2. Depending on how your breath was to start with, begin to intentionally bring the pattern back to a level place. Breathe in either through your nose or open mouth deeply, pause, and then exhale very deliberately through your mouth. If it's helpful for you to do a mental count, try and exhale for a second or two longer than you inhale.

3. As you breathe, you can affirm to yourself in your mind that whatever is happening to overwhelm you is a temporary experience (because it is).

4. Take note of your body beginning to relax and shift when you focus only on your breath.

No matter what the problem, try and remind yourself that on the most primal level you are a feral creature that requires breath to rebalance and regroup. Give yourself this gift as an act of powerful self-care.

Laugh Wildly

Have you ever laughed deep from your soul? The kind of laughter where you probably look ugly as hell, are struggling to breathe, and are in a near-transcendent space of true joy? Wild laughter, the kind that is completely out of your control, is one of the most incredible of human experiences. It's like being utterly possessed with the spirit of joy. If you've experienced this, then you'll know it is a top-notch experience and one that can be medicine for your domesticated and overworked soul.

Laughing is scientifically proven to be good for human beings, which is why it's a must when discussing self-care. When we laugh, our brains release pleasure chemicals, such as endorphins, and the physical act of laughing can help with heart health and blood flow. However, when going feral we are not just talking *any* laughing here; we're talking the kind of laugh that is coming from the unhinged, impolite depths of your soul. The type of laughter where you don't care how obnoxiously loud you are or if you're braying like a donkey. The type of laughter where you fully let go!

Letting go is fundamental to your well-being, but it can feel tempting to do everything you can to avoid it. In the human world, we are under constant pressure to look a certain way, act a certain way, to be polite, tame, and fit into assigned roles and boxes (e.g., being a "nice guy/girl" or "good employee"). There are few times and spaces where you may feel the freedom to just be. To let the feral little gremlin within yourself be ugly, silly, wild, and free. To succumb to the wild laugh is to let yourself relax and release.

Given the information overload faced in current society, it can seem like there isn't a lot of shit to have a carefree laugh about. The world is a beautiful place, but it can feel cold, mean, and desolate at times. However, humor heals, and every moment you spend laughing in joy is medicine for your spirit, which in turn brings light to the world. The entire human experience is about taking it all in, the good and the bad, succumbing to this life as a sensory and emotional experience!

Sometimes it just ain't so serious.

So your feral self-care task is this: Allow yourself to get caught up in the realm of the wild laugh! Let it take you over and carry you away to a space where joy vibrates through you, body *and* soul.

How to Do It

Although the wild laugh is something that tends to happen spontaneously in the right circumstances, there are things you can do to try and coax it out. For example:

- Watch one of your favorite comedians perform.
- Spend time with someone who typically brings you joy.
- Watch a movie or video that you know puts you into hysterics.
- Do something that breaks social norms but is fun in the process (for example, many of the entries in this very book!).
- Do something exhilarating and physical.
- Try an activity that is messy and fun.
- Play like a child.

Whatever you choose, the vital component is that you will be able to let go. To this end, you should be somewhere (and/or with someone) that makes you feel completely comfortable and free to be yourself. We're talking a completely unhinged attitude toward whether you snort, wheeze, pee, or drool. The wild laugh is medicine, so give yourself a dose!

Immerse Yourself in Water

In conversations about self-care there is one thing that makes every list and every article, spawning an industry of products to help boost the soothing rewards: the bath! It's the quintessential example of taking care of yourself and has become almost synonymous with self-care itself. This is well earned too, as baths have a myriad of both physical and mental health benefits. They can soothe the body, relieve stress, and allow you to carve out some much-needed quiet time in the fuckery and noise of being a modern-day person.

However, if you examine the bath on a deeper level, it isn't just about the tub, the warm water, or the nice-smelling products that are doing the trick. For human beings, immersing the body in water has been something that has had both spiritual and mundane significance throughout history. On a spiritual level, water is associated with emotion and purity. And although you use it to literally cleanse your body, it can feel emotionally and spiritually cleansing as well to symbolically allow the water to wash away the drama and bad vibes so you can emerge feeling cleansed and refreshed. Whether it be in natural sources, such as waterfalls or lakes, or in intentionally created pools and tubs, the modern predilection for baths is a carryover from ancestral behavior and remains significant to life and culture to this day!

Looking at it from a primal perspective: All humans developed in the watery cocoon of the mother's womb. It's no wonder that being immersed in water has become an icon of safety, relaxation, and loving care. And you don't need to have all the smelly products or a *Pinterest*-perfect setup in order to gain the benefits. Your animal body still gets some powerful feral self-care whether you are immersing yourself in the stream of the shower, in a lake, in natural hot springs, or any other water source. The joyful and wild creature within you would delight to even run in the rain or frolic in puddles!

So although the feral self-care ethos is all about breaking the stereotypes when it comes to self-care, the act of immersing yourself in water is such a vital part of healing and care that this more mainstream practice is one that can stay!

How to Do It

How to approach this depends on what sort of access you have to a water source. The secret to getting the feral self-care benefits from this task is in sinking into the *experience* itself. Whether you are in a tub, shower, or lake, the steps are simple:

1. Begin by getting in the water and just experiencing it fully through your animal body in a mindfully present way. How does it feel? What is the temperature? What sounds are present? What is the movement of the water?
2. Imagine that all the chaotic garbage that you've accumulated as a modern human is melting away or being washed off you. Conceptualize the water as cleansing and protecting you. Visualize this while still keeping present in experiencing the *sensation* of the water.
3. After this practice, take note of how you feel, and thank your body.

Slither and Stretch

These animal bodies of ours are amazing; however, they can also be a prime pain in the ass. They're notoriously finicky, require a lot of upkeep and care, and break down easily without some routine maintenance! Sadly, many people don't give their bodies the kind of medicinal movement they need to work at their best. The kind of movement humans as a species evolved for—the movement that was the basis of life pre-modernity. In the modern context, most spend a lot of life sedentary or completely hunched over. Your poor spine is often arched over your laptop, your phone, or little pots of ice cream at 3 a.m. (no judgment). The average life today has nowhere near the amount of movement your feral creature body needs in order to work, and feel, its best.

Self-care isn't just about soothing your mind and spirit. It's also about being your own mechanic when it comes to this meat suit you operate and doing the responsible things necessary to kick that bitch into prime working condition. A simple place to start is to take up stretching.

Stretching out your body and muscles is known to have a variety of practical physical health benefits. Not only can it relieve tension and help with acute injuries or pain, but it can also be a form of preventative care. Those who stretch more often are less likely to suffer from accidental pulls and strains. Apart from that, it just *feels* good. To slither and stretch, moving your animal body in a way that is soothing and relaxing, can improve blood flow and circulation, simultaneously making your brain shoot out pleasurable chemicals, such as endorphins.

This shit just *feels good*!

Just because the domestication of the human species has reduced your need to move doesn't mean that this has been in your best interest. Taking care of your creature form is an important part of self-care. After all, this body is the portal through which you get to experience life. Stretching is a low-impact, high-reward way to do this while helping you feel good in the process!

How to Do It

Stretching can be done at any point during the day, but it can be an especially relaxing and soothing way to both start and end the day. When stretching, you can boost the feral self-care returns by pairing it with other activities from this book. For example, you can:

- Stretch outside.
- Stretch in a sunbeam.
- Stretch while deep breathing.
- Stretch as part of a sensory wake-up.
- Follow a stretch with a primal scream.

As you go through different stretching positions, pause each one for a few seconds (if it feels good and safe to do so) then release. You can even "shake it out" by flailing your body and limbs if that feels good for you after. The purpose is just to give your animal body the opportunity to move in a way that works for you.

Given the fact that most people are far more sedentary than their primal ancestors, the most important thing here is safety. Although stretching sounds very gentle and Zen, there is definitely the possibility of doing too much too fast and injuring yourself. As with most things, the key to success can be found in the intersection of taking it slow and listening to your body.

Do a Sensory Shake-Up

In today's world, it can be easy to slip into a trance of disconnection. Not just a disconnect from the natural world but a disconnect from *living* itself. For many, attempting to keep sane through the pressures of modern-day life can be all-consuming, and there isn't much time and energy left on the fringes to truly experience a wild and free life.

Your animal body longs to feel connected, not only with the natural world but with the primal felt experience of life itself. The human experience is not meant to be spent sitting hunched over computers all day, trapped in the realm of the mind. You are meant to be living with gusto, recklessly enjoying life through the portal of this human form.

Our species has evolved to be stingy with our awareness and attention. Although we assume we are fully present and aware of our surroundings, research shows that we actually attend to only so many stimuli while our brains fill in the rest. It's only when there is something that truly wrangles your attention (like physical discomfort or the presence of a bad smell) that our awareness reconnects to the body, shifting our attention and awareness once more. However, we all have the option to mindfully "wake up" our sensory systems in an intentional, deliberate way. Doing so can shake us out of autopilot so we can fully experience sensory input and be present in our bodies.

How to Do It

The next time you are in a situation where you are feeling overwhelmed with anxiety or like you've been floating on autopilot, do this exercise to shake up and wake up your senses.

What you need:
- Something scented in a handheld size (e.g., a candle, a cup of hot coffee, or a flower).
- Something with a sharp taste (e.g., a mint, sour candy, or fresh fruit).

Steps:

1. Stand or sit somewhere comfortable and cross your arms, placing each hand on the opposite upper arm (think a self-hug).
2. Pay close attention to the feeling of your arms beneath your palms and take three to six deep breaths. Tap all of your fingers on your upper arms as you would drum on a tabletop, and state aloud to yourself, "Wake up, touch."
3. Then shake out your arms and upper body.
4. Return to awareness of your breathing, then pay attention to what sounds you hear.
5. Knock on a hard surface and pay keen attention to the sound and where it is felt in your body. State aloud to yourself, "Wake up, hearing."
6. Keep taking deep breaths and inhale slowly and deliberately. Grab your scented item, inhale slowly and deliberately, and state aloud to yourself, "Wake up, smell."
7. Take your edible item and place it in your mouth. Pay attention to how it tastes, and let the flavor and sensation of what you're eating bloom in your mouth. State aloud to yourself, "Wake up, taste."
8. Place your hands over your eyes for a minute or so. Then move your hands and look at your body and at your surroundings. Zoom in if you want to the texture of your skin or to the usually overlooked details of the things around you. State aloud to yourself, "Wake up, sight."
9. Shake out your arms and exhale messily, trying to literally shake up your body system.

How did it feel to wake up your senses?

Find Physical Catharsis

A large part of feral self-care is connecting your awareness to the felt sensations in the body. Although it may seem like just a problematic meat suit riddled with obnoxious needs and random ailments, your body holds so much wisdom and guidance—when you choose to listen. It is an incredible machine that helps you process emotion. Through medicinal movement and grounding yourself in the physical, you become more capable of processing and moving through difficult mental or emotional things, transmuting that energy into something that is more supportive to you.

Modern stress varies considerably from the kinds of crises people faced in the past. For your ancestors, the stress response evolved from being faced with predators and as a motivator for survival. The fight or flight response literally allowed the body to be supercharged and activated to, well, fight or flee! The modern iteration of this response is so dramatically different in context that it's borderline absurd. You can have these mental and physical crisis reactions flooding your system at any moment, whether in the bread aisle of the grocery store or simply sitting on your couch. The problem with this is that unlike your ancestors who had to take action in order to survive the threat they faced, you aren't (usually) required to *do* something to move that energy *through* and *out* of you. You can survive without facing this stress response head-on.

But there is more to life than just surviving. Instead of trying to ignore them or wish them away, you can take all those grimy feelings and release them through a physical channel. You need a way to let the demons out—the murky, yucky feelings, such as anxiety, anger, fear, and overwhelm, that will build and loom if not released. Sadly,

modern couch-potato culture doesn't afford the same organic opportunities for purposeful, cathartic release like fighting or fleeing, so it
is up to you to give those opportunities to yourself. As a sweaty treat!

So your next feral self-care assignment is this: Find something
purposeful and physically cathartic to do that can help you move negative energy through and out of you. Channel the bullshit in order to
move past it, engaging your primal animal body as a powerful form of
physical self-care.

How to Do It

For some people, going to the gym to exercise may accomplish this
goal of releasing negative energy. However, from a feral perspective, you need something more strenuous and primal. Something to
unleash your inner monster!

Here are some examples of ways to get the evil out that are fun
and feral:

- Chopping wood.
- Fighting a punching bag.
- Sprinting/running.
- Climbing trees.
- Building things.
- Smashing things.

The important thing is to find something productive that will satisfy that urge for physical catharsis and release.

Now, obviously, this task should be attempted safely within your
own ability and skill level. Let's not have any broken backs or strained
shoulders up in this bitch. Make sure you're stretched, hydrated, and
are listening to your body throughout the process.

Engage in Mindful Cleaning

As a neurodivergent adult with multiple competing priorities, I often find myself easily overwhelmed with chores. As the saying goes, "An ounce of prevention is worth a pound of cure"; however, sometimes the mess gets out of hand before I have the time or mental energy to deal with it. Suddenly there is a pile-up of responsibilities that feels bigger than my capacity to tackle it. Sound familiar?

It is no secret that many modern humans have mental health issues to cope with. This can be immensely challenging when also participating in a capitalist civilization where you need financial resources to survive. Instead of dealing with mental health recovery like you would recover from physical ailments such as surgery, you can end up in a place of needing to "keep on keeping on"—pretending everything is okay so you can get by.

I'm a firm believer that your environment has a huge impact on your mental health. While you are in no way required to keep some spotless clean house to maintain a healthy mental state, it can be incredibly difficult to clean up your mental state when there's an endless list of chores that need to be done. Your spaces may be a visual reflection of how you feel inside: chaotic and cluttered. These spaces can also be a major trigger for more guilt, shame, and anxiety.

One of the best ways to cope with this issue is to engage in mindful cleaning. Mindful cleaning is an exercise where you don't focus on the mess itself but on the felt experience of approaching the cleanup. For example, lighting candles, putting on some fun music, or doing tasks that allow yourself to get lost in the physical sensation of what you're doing. This can act as a remedy for overwhelm, as the task is not solely to clean the house or achieve anything in particular. It's mainly about using the opportunity to find some self-care in the act of being physically present while having the bonus side effect of getting shit done. Doing the dishes by hand is a great example, as it can be an incredibly effective way of jolting yourself out of a mental spiral and helping unlock the feral self-care that comes with becoming grounded again in your physical body.

How to Do It

1. The first step for mindful cleaning is to be aware of what mindfulness feels like in the first place. Place a hand on a table and just focus on how that feels. What is the texture? The temperature? This is the kind of focus and attention you will be bringing to your to-do list.

2. Next, pick something that needs to be done. Something small that is not overwhelming that seems like it would have sensory returns. For example, when washing the dishes, you get to experience a myriad of sensations. The heat, the bubbles, the scrubbing—oh my! You may never have realized what a multisensory extravaganza this task was until you started paying attention to it!

3. For other tasks that may not have such a clear sensory element, get creative with making it a sensory experience for yourself. Lighting scented candles that are designated for mindful cleaning, using the task as a specified time to listen to a favorite podcast or music: There are many possibilities to make this a chance to drop the pressure and zone into the task at hand.

CHAPTER 4

Chaos and Creativity:
LIBERATING YOURSELF THROUGH CREATIVE EXPRESSION AND PLAY

Leaning way into chaos and creativity is key for unleashing some powerful feral self-care. Think messy play, inner child healing, lollygagging, and just general aimless screwing around! These are all vital forms of magic that spark joy and fun. Your primal nature longs for this—to be wildly unhinged, to roll with life's punches, to create (not necessarily with purpose), and to make life's challenges your playground. And honestly, you have one life, might as well have a blast with it!

This chapter is all about indulging our creative impulses in order to find some messy, creative self-care. After all, creativity is one of the things that sets humans apart. Artistic merits aside, you are constantly creating your world and your perceptions of it as you move through life. Use this to your advantage and let your inner goblin loose to play, create, innovate, and generally mess around in order to find the natural flow. By cozying up to chaos and creativity, you will become more resilient, have more fun, and find some self-care that's as uniquely unhinged as you are!

Make an Emotional Mess

It cannot be stated enough: Your mind does not have the capacity to comfortably hold the drama and the bullshit of life. You need to regularly channel this energy into something less prickly and heavy, allowing your body to act as a physical medium for reworking all that messy mind stuff into something that feels a little lighter to hold.

One of the most primal ways to approach this task is through art. The ability to turn thought and feeling into various art forms is a hallmark of the human species, and it is both healing and fulfilling. Although "art" can look like a great many things, the modalities that tap into unhinged imagination and messy play and that incorporate the felt sensations of the body are of vital concern when it comes to feral self-care.

For this reason, finger painting is a delightfully messy approach to the task of transmuting your mental mess. Similar to rolling a stress ball through your fingers, to finger paint is to engage the body in a tactile strategy for working through difficult feelings and feeling more grounded again. In modern adulthood, people don't get the same opportunities as children to play in the realms of sticky, gloopy, messy creativity. But by pairing art making with this felt sensory experience, you can kill two birds with one stone—and reap all the feral self-care rewards while doing so.

In keeping with the feral self-care ethos, truly let yourself sink into the sticky, mucky feeling of this messy task. Does it disgust or titillate you? Good. As with most things unhinged and creative, this is an intuitive endeavor. Do not be concerned with pretty, civilized ideas about what you could create that would be impressive or welcomed by others. This is artistic goblin mode; there is just as juicy self-care goodness to be squeezed out of a result that looks like a brownish blob of chaos as there is in a frame-worthy piece.

How to Do It

If the concept of intuitive finger-paint art is truly foreign to you, then here are some prompts to get you started:

1. What colors are your feelings? What do these colors mean to you personally?
2. What shapes are your feelings taking? In which way are your fingers being "pulled" to tell a story?
3. Are you finding yourself concerned about how it will look?
4. Are you okay with the colors blending and letting go of an aesthetic end result?

If you are familiar with color theory psychology, you can use this knowledge to direct the emotive mess you make. Color psychology looks at how different colors influence human behavior and emotion and what these colors typically represent. However, this knowledge is not required, as *you* are your best guide. When approaching this task intuitively, allow yourself to be guided by what these colors mean for you personally.

Once completed, you can continue to work with the emotive mess you've made by reflecting on the experience. How does it feel to have translated your feelings into something tangible? Can you see any hidden pictures or symbols in your work? What did the process feel like and what would you do differently next time?

Indulge In a Fantasy

Human beings have many superpowers, one of which is the ability to use imagination as a manifesting machine! You may find yourself taking this power for granted because it operates subtly behind awareness. But when you truly stop to think about it, how cool is it that you are able to dream things up and then funnel them into the realm of tangible reality using only your mind, creativity, and some good ol' human ingenuity?

In many cases it all starts with a daydream. The infancy of all tangible human creation begins in the realm of thought. In modern human capitalist society, to daydream is often viewed negatively as a detriment—like some flaky, out-of-touch quality that spits in the face of the almighty goal of productivity above all else! But when you understand the imagination-to-action pipeline, you get a firm grasp that all productivity must *first* start with the seed of imagination. Even your to-do list was a fragment of thought before it was something you could hold.

From a feral self-care standpoint, you must allow yourself to daydream. Your primal self longs to soak up the benefits of aimless creative thought and fantasy, not only so you can be more productive but foremost to take a break from the limitations of reality and feel the delicious, refreshing taste of escape! Your human nature is best honored by spending time with a foot in *both* realms; sometimes it is the best act of feral self-care to sink into the experience of your body, and sometimes it's best for you to indulge the uniquely human ability to travel beyond the physical into the realm of fantasy and creative thought.

How to Do It

Now, you might be an avid daydreamer already. If so, great job, and keep that shit up! If you aren't, take up the challenge to find some self-care in the act of allowing your thoughts to carry you away from the present reality (obviously when it is safe to do so). To do this, find a nice spot to sit or lie down. Turn off any devices so you won't be distracted, then just...well...let your mind wander!

Here are some simple prompts to get you started in daydreaming:

- What are your goals and dreams?
- What are your desires?
- Can you build an imaginary "safe space"? What's in it?
- What would be pleasant or pleasurable to be experiencing right now?
- What is a recurring fantasy for you?

Alternatively, you can ditch the prompts and simply grab on to the kite of imaginative consciousness. Where are your thoughts taking *you*? What ride are you going to go on if you let go and just allow yourself to be carried?

Ultimately, the goal is to give yourself permission to play in this space of infinite possibility and intuitive creative chaos. To indulge in fantasy is to give yourself a self-care gift that has a deeper impact than any pedicure or bath bomb. More than just idle mind wandering, daydreaming is the medicinal break your brain sorely needs to reset *and* come up with your next great idea.

Engage in Chaotic Symphony

For as long as humans have been humaning, they have been making music! Whether for entertainment, spirituality, or social time, there are a variety of ways that music has had deep meaning for the species and a fundamental role in culture. Playing with the concepts of sound and vibration, people have blended imagination, voice, and rhythmically beating on whatever they can with their hands and bodies as a way to enrich their lives throughout the ages. On a primal level, music is deeply important to humans. Not just the appreciation of it, but the desire and urge to participate experimentally and play in the realm of sound. As a form of self-expression, it is healing, cathartic, and has a primal impact on the senses.

Music is a creative tool and outlet for emotional release. As you go through life's trials and tribulations, you can become energetically swamped with all sorts of emotional baggage. Sometimes all that energy gets stuck within your body and it yearns to be free! There are many ways to find release, and one is to do so musically. Like most creative endeavors, skill level doesn't necessarily need to come into play here. Music is simply a creative release valve available to everyone!

Human culture can feel incredibly limiting when it comes to freedom of expression. All too often you can be put in situations where you are expected to sit down and shut up. Stay small, be polite, and don't step out of line. However, deep within your feral soul there is an untamed creature that longs to make noise, to go wild, and to freely express itself in whichever way feels good in the moment! It is a high act of love to your authenticity to give yourself an outlet of expression, and music is just one way you can do this while also fulfilling your creative needs.

So if you want to embrace your wild in a way that is creative and free, then look no further than creating your own chaotic symphony! Let loose by channeling your creative and emotional energy into the playful realm of sound. You do not need any formal instruments or training for this, just the desire to indulge and the understanding that music is a tool for your feral self-care through and through.

How to Do It

When the urge strikes, take any pent-up, restless energy and indulge the desire to create music and play with sound using whatever you have available. While some people may have access to instruments, this isn't necessary. After all, your body and voice are instruments! Sticks, spoons, or tables can be instruments! Music can be pulled from the imagination space and given birth here with whatever you have available.

Some examples of things that can work for your chaotic symphony are:

- Banging on pots and pans.
- Putting on shoes and imitation tap dancing on a hardwood floor.
- Playing your cutlery like drums along countertops or the edges of the sink.
- Breaking into wordless song, such as humming, vocal toning, or chanting sounds.

Begin experimenting with the sounds and take note of what you like and what you don't like. What makes your spine tingle and what's a full-body "fuck no." Shake up the rhythm. Pay close attention to the thoughts that come; are these sounds sad, joyful, or simply just noise? As with all feral self-care, there are no right or wrong answers, just simple sensations and the indulgence of being primally, beautifully in the moment.

Collect Trinkets and Treasures

Ahhh, the human urge to hoard shit! It seems that deep within most humans is a greedy little goblin that loves to collect. You can see evidence of this going way back in history, with archaeological sites being littered with all sorts of trinkets, gems, and meaningful objects. It seems an appreciation for trinkets, shinies, and treasures is a desire that's evolved with our species throughout time.

Even now, you can see this urge in action when watching children. If you've ever been on a walk with a child, then chances are you've witnessed the gleeful stuffing of pockets with flowers, rocks, and sticks, oh my! Kids just love to collect things that bring them joy for whatever reason. Sometimes it's about the aesthetics, and other times they can't really tell *what* exactly it is that they're drawn to. All they seem to know is that they've gotta have it!

Although accumulating piles and piles of joyless crap you don't need is draining on the human spirit, collecting things you love can actually be beneficial for your well-being. Your wee goblin brain churns out the happy chemicals when you indulge in this primal urge to collect *all the things*! And indulging the childlike urge to gather things that tickle your senses is a way to feel freedom in the tight embrace of modern adulthood. In some cases, collecting can even help you socially, allowing you to find community with like-minded collectors, providing a much-needed social common ground that can be fulfilling and fun.

One way to liberate your authenticity is to let go of any societal expectations and let yourself find joy in the simple act of collecting things. Channel your inner magpie and find pleasure in surrounding yourself with trinkets that are meaningful to *you*. These collections don't have to make sense to anyone else, and they certainly don't need to be explained. Maybe they look good, or maybe they have good vibes. Whatever the reason may be, to hoard and collect things is part of your human nature, and to indulge this urge can be a fun and quirky act of feral self-care.

So lean into the goblin urge to intuitively collect and display things that bring you joy. Surround yourself intentionally with the vibes you want to call in.

How to Do It

Take an intuitive approach to curating collections of things you enjoy. Start by taking any thoughts of what's "acceptable" to collect and surround yourself with and throwing them in the trash (within reason!). Truly play and explore with the idea of what it is that makes *you* happy. After all, that's the point: to be happy in your own spaces and life.

You only have one life—you might as well spend it surrounded by the weird shit you love!

Try Magical Play

In the modern era, adult humans are not encouraged to make the time to seek magic. Despite the fact that we still carry a deep desire for it. Magic is truly all around. It's in myths, media, and still present in the make-believe of children. But somewhere along the line, many people ceased to engage in magical play, trading it in in exchange for the responsibilities of adulthood and the cloistering limitations of taking reality at face value.

It's a bad deal!

I don't give a fuck how old you are. As a child of the wild, you have the right to reclaim your magic. Indulging in magical play is not just for children and witches. It's for anyone who wants to reclaim the mystical and playful aspect of themselves and reject the idea that adulthood is devoid of magic. To reclaim your magic as a human being is to reclaim your humanity itself.

There is something deep within you that longs for the magical play you enjoyed when you were a child. To create wands from sticks, form habits into meaningful rituals, and play with plants to make potions. This is the kind of chaos and creativity that nourishes our primal human nature. How did society get to a space where magical play seems "out there" but putting on pants and going to work cosplaying as a "functional adult" doesn't? Who's making the rules around here? Because everything is backward!

If you want some feral self-care that honors your humanity and gives you the space to go wildly creative with the concepts of possibility and play, then get back to playing with magic.

How to Do It

There are a variety of ways to lean into magical play. In fact, you may have memories of what to do based on what you did when you were a child. However, if you are unsure, the following is an example of a way to bring magical play into your feral self-care: Make a magical wand.

Go out on a nature walk or hike and look for a stick that is the right size and shape to act as a wand. This is an intuitive call and not something that should require too much thought or energy. Once you find this wand, bring it home and dress it up however you please. Some people will love it best when left alone, while others may want to shave off the bark, paint it, or hot glue meaningful things to it. In keeping with the ethos of feral self-care, lean into whatever you feel is the right way to go!

Once you have your wand, decide some things you want to do with it. Open your mind a wee bit and lean into some magical thinking and imaginative play. If this *was* magic (which it *absolutely is* if you choose), what would you point it at and to what end? Some suggestions:

- Point it at your laundry piles to invoke the motivation to fold and put them away!
- Point it at your bank balance in hopes of some unexpected deposit!
- Point it at the mirror to get your shit-talking in order!

As with most things feral self-care, the magic is in the doing. Allow yourself to lean into the spirit of magic and imagination as a form of creative expression and feral rejuvenation.

Build a Blanket Fort

When it comes to feral self-care, few things top the feeling of a full-body rejection of what it means to be a "proper grownup." To conform to this tight-laced idea of what adulthood "should" be makes the feral possum within you hiss in displeasure! Part of going feral is to embrace the chaotic inner child within. If you are a grownup who's always struggled to fit in the mold of what an "adult person" should be, chances are your connection to this inner wild thing is especially strong.

This is a superpower!

Being a grownup is hard AF; just take a look around for the proof! A great way to escape (at least temporarily) is to indulge that inner feral wildling that just wants to play, create, and hide from the pressures of modern-day life. Long gone are the days when we had to huddle in caves as a form of shelter; however, the desire to curl up in cozy corners never left. There is a primitive urge within you to hide as a form of protection, enjoying the chance to be sheltered from whatever's plaguing you. Although in modern times you may not be in a space of needing to hide away from large predators, there still are other things that give you the urge to burrow inward. For example, the pressure to be constantly vigilant and responsible for worrying about *all the things*!

So your feral self-care assignment is this: Bring the healing energy of the archetypal cave into your grown-up life in the form of adult blanket forting! Enjoy the act of creating your own soft little sanctuary, just as you did as a kid. Not only does this satisfy the primal urge to burrow as self-care, but it also satisfies the urges you still carry as an adult to get creative and take a little pause from the pressures of life. Think of this: At some point as a child, you made your last blanket fort without even realizing it, then carried on into adulthood as if that had to be left behind. A tragic error that you have the power to remedy!

How to Do It

To make your own DIY adult blanket fort, all you need is some blankets or bed sheets, household items or structures to help keep them in place (such as books, chairs, couches, or tables), and your own crotchety desire to retreat from society altogether!

To begin, gather your supplies. You can simply arrange the household items or structures in a way so that when you lay the blankets or sheets over them, you create a little hidey-hole to tuck into. Heavier items, such as books, can be used to strengthen your fort by holding down your textiles. Alternatively, you can go all out by planning your structure a little more carefully and using clothesline, rope or string, and clips or clothespins to affix your blankets in a way that creates a cozy little space that will fit at least one unhinged adult human comfortably.

The essence of the blanket fort is coziness. To supercharge this, feel free to add more blankets, pillows, or other soft furnishings. Additional add-ons include flameless LED candles (no fire hazards, please), fairy lights, soft music, journals, or whatever your heart desires! The important thing is to approach this in the spirit of comfort and play. There is no good reason that blanket forts get left behind in childhood. Adulthood is hard; help soften the experience with cozy textiles and your own comfy space to retreat.

Play Pretend

People may act as if being detached from reality is a bad thing, but have you looked around lately? *Yikes!* The truth is that reality can be overwhelming, and everyone could use a break from it from time to time. As a human being, you have a very special and unique ability: to engage in the realm of the pretend. To do so is to honor the curious and playful creator that lies in your human nature!

While children are encouraged to play pretend, as it is beneficial for development, adults are not often afforded the opportunity or encouragement to do so. Whether it be constraints of time or energy (i.e., if there's enough available after a long day of modern human-ing) or a matter of self-consciousness (worrying about how it affects your standing as a "proper grownup"), at some point along the line most people put a lid on the amount of time spent in the realm of the pretend.

However, this imagination space is not an idle zone of the unreal: It is a sprawling, expansive space of creation and endless possibility! Pretend play allows you to explore the world around you more deeply. It helps you to process things, play with hypotheticals, and experiment. By approaching this practice as an adult with intentionality and openness, you can find yourself happier and more connected to a fundamental part of your human nature.

It's a beautiful act of feral self-care to indulge in pretend play. To recognize that this is a superpower of the human species that can be used to your benefit. Reality can feel very limiting, busy, and full of heavy responsibilities. Pretend play can be a soothing balm to these pressures.

How to Do It

There are a variety of ways to engage in pretend play as a form of feral self-care. However, something that can be really useful is using role-play. As a human being, you carry an innate desire to explore through role-play and can slip into this kind of imagining intuitively.

Role-playing can be many things, but to get you started, you can think of it as exploring what it would be like to be someone (or something) else. For example, sometimes I like to role-play as one of those mythical people who actually has their shit together (as if!). Role-playing can also be the act of "playing out" how you would act in certain situations, such as a date or job interview. This is a prime opportunity to take a break from your ego "self" and to play around with something else. Maybe it's an animal. Maybe it's the qualities, characteristics, or "vibe" of someone you admire. There are endless ways to approach imaginative play through role-playing.

In feral self-care terms, it can be immensely cathartic to role-play in ways that let your most authentic and uncivilized self free. Anything that lets you play without judgment or act in ways that are messy, ugly, or wild. When you try this out, you may find yourself feeling equal parts exhilarated and deeply connected to the primal animal within (even if it has been buried under many years of domestication and social conditioning). So play pretend and do so often: The more opportunities you give yourself to connect with your inner feral creature, the greater the fulfillment and authenticity you can get.

Sing Your Surroundings

Singing has been a way for humans to express themselves since the beginning of time. You can touch something truly transcendent when channeling emotion through vocal release. Whether it be a sad song or a joyous, lilting ballad, to sing is something that is deeply and primally human. And like most endeavors that are creative in nature, the benefit from singing is not exclusive to skill level. Even the most tone-deaf among us can glean the benefits of participating in song!

Human beings are fantastic at recognizing patterns, and your brain is hardwired in a way that is inherently creative. This is why you are drawn to song and can suss out the musicality in even the most mundane sounds (like when you notice a sort of protomusical beat in the sound of traffic). As a creative machine, you also have the power to generate song, which leads to many playful opportunities to break into song as a way to delight and entertain yourself.

This is one of the things that is beautifully and primally human: to play and create in a way that is wholly tied to being in the moment. In your wildest state, you carry the urge to play, to be silly, and to just be...wherever that may take you. While it's true that your primal ancestors had to take very seriously the simple task of just *surviving*, for many modern humans, this life of convenience should at the very least afford you a little time and energy left to be silly, engage in fun and shenanigans, and to fuck around as a form of authentically fulfilling self-care!

So your next feral self-care task is to use the power of song as a form of release and creative self-expression. Throw out any and every concern about doing this skillfully or in a way that is palatable. To get in touch with the feral goblin within you, throw out those concerns in favor of more important ones: How does it feel to sing in this wild way? Are you indulging impulse? Are you satisfying the urge to be completely unhinged?

How to Do It

To begin, choose a lame, mundane task in your life that *has* to be done and make it an exercise in fun and creative joy by pairing it with spontaneous song. For example, cleaning or organizing your taxes. Although you can achieve the feral self-care benefits of this task by singing whatever you choose as you work, I personally find I get the most self-care bang for my buck when belting out what it is I'm actually *doing*. The absurdity of such a thing is equal parts fun and hysterical, and it's truly hard to maintain a shitty attitude toward whatever chore you're tackling when behaving in such a way.

In the simple act of indulging the instinct to break into song, you can satisfy something that is deeply and primally human while inviting some feral fun into your modern-day life!

Create a Shit List

In the modern world of social media, fakery has become fashionable. It can often feel like we're all just in some race to show off an amazing house, picture-perfect family, and gains from success. It's become far too easy to compare yourself to the world's online population in an instant, and the "highlight" reel has become some bonkers caricature of reality. We also live in a timeline where toxic positivity runs rampant, the idea that you can positively think your way out of your problems. While mindset is a huge factor in happiness, the raw, unfiltered truth is that you have to acknowledge the bad shit in order to move forward.

Sometimes you need to let yourself truly roll around in the messy unpleasantness of your own humanity. After all, that's part of what it is to go feral. To become untamed and wildly authentic—even if it isn't pretty or palatable to some. There is no need to pretend that you are above the petty, nasty little urges that reside within you. Sometimes it's absolutely better to just let yourself wallow in your childish and dark feelings, letting them move through you so you can shut them down in a timely manner, moving forward a little lighter, with your head held high.

Self-care absolutely includes having a wee wallow, even if it's not the "polite" thing to do. Human beings can naturally fall into these messy mental states, and although you need to be careful of lingering on them too long, there is no problem with taking the time to bitch and complain, to vent and moan, and to acknowledge that sometimes things just suck!

So let it all out, baby! If you're pissy, frustrated, upset, jealous, or prickly and need a release from pretending everything is fine or carrying the burden of those feelings in silence, let them loose!

How to Do It

Take a deep breath, put pen to paper, and allow all the shitty thoughts and feelings to move through you. The petty complaints; the whiny, foot-stomping grievances; the laundry list of people, places, or things that are chapping your ass today. Let them flow from your mental mess onto the paper, where they can no longer take up space in your heart, mind, or energy. Get it all out and carry on your merry way.

For best results, rip up the list after writing it and exhale with a primal grunt or growl. Destroy that evidence! Although it can be a cathartic experience for you to get it out, it could be jarring to have anybody actually see this list, so tear it, crush it, or (safely) burn it.

Most importantly, truly release the drama and try and have as much unhinged fun as possible. A good motto to live by is "throw yourself a pity party, but give yourself a curfew," meaning take the time to wallow, but cut it off when it's no longer helpful.

Additional ideas to approach writing this list in the spirit of unhinged levity include:

- Scribbling pictures in the margins.
- Drawing a small chart outlining the levels of suckage in specific life areas.
- Writing a small poem about your grievances then reciting it aloud in a silly voice.
- Peeking at an online insult generator (may I suggest the Shakespearean version?) to really give your list some flair.

Stress is toxic for your body and spirit, so by approaching your troubles with fun and a little uncivilized creativity, you are giving your messy humanity the sweet medicine of some feral self-care.

Practice Freewriting

To engage in purposeless creativity is a beautifully productive thing. If people released the idea that our creations have to be palatable or for public consumption, everyone would be free to tap into that dimension of themselves more fully. Sometimes I like to conceptualize this by placing my sense of self outside of the rest of reality: If I were the only human being on this planet, outside of any civilization or influence, how would I approach creation? How would I allow creative expression to flow if the only metric of success available was personal fulfillment?

One tool that is very beneficial for tapping into this stream of raw creativity is freewriting. Freewriting is the act of simply writing without a specified topic or purpose and letting what comes out, come out! Freewriting allows the subconscious, intuition, and *whatever else* (the creative muse, perhaps?) to come through and take the wheel. In many cases, it can act as a valuable window, showing you what may be lurking in the depths of your animal brain when logic and purpose are kept out of the equation. In many cases, it can also act as a form of release. For example, when freewriting, you may find yourself channeling difficult emotions or hashing out internal problems that you are grappling with.

From a feral self-care perspective, freewriting is not only valuable for embracing undeveloped creative impulse but can also help give you the opportunity to sift through the mental clutter that's specific to the modern world. For most, life is filled with multiple competing priorities. There is a near-constant barrage of things to think about, responsibilities to carry out, problems to solve, and the random flashes of ideas and opinions that noisily intrude into the corners of awareness. In addition, there is also the mental noise that accumulates from your interactions with other people and engaging with endless streams of content online. This creates a cacophony of chaos that's loud in both an energetic and mental sense.

With all of this input, it can be difficult for you to hear and connect with yourself. Your intuition, your desires, the wisdom of your animal body. So you are tasked with the challenge of finding ways to tap back in, in order to get back to a space of balance. Freewriting can allow you to take on this challenge while also tickling that human instinct to create just for the sake of it.

How to Do It

To initiate a freewriting session, set yourself up somewhere comfy with comfort trinkets, sounds, textures, or smells nearby. There are really no rules to freewriting other than putting pen to paper and allowing yourself to act as the conduit for whatever chooses to emerge.

Put any silly ideas of judgment aside and just allow yourself to channel out whatever flows. Will it be a poem? Word salad? Doodles? A lengthy list of grievances? Whatever it is, just let it move through you and release it by putting pen to paper.

Whether it gives complete unreadable nonsense or is a complex dissertation on how to solve your problems, you've done a great job in just the simple act of engaging with this enterprise. Regardless of whatever does or does not happen in a freewriting session, it is *always* time well spent.

Create Unhinged Affirmations

It's well established that cleaning up your self-talk is a fundamental aspect of self-care. As you shape-shift from child to adult, you pick up a lot of ideas and beliefs about yourself that become folded into a robust inner monologue that either cheers you on or tears you down. This inner voice is one that never shuts the hell up, and you have little to no escape from it (aside from perhaps sleeping or drowning your sorrows in whatever mind-numbing agent is on the menu). However, challenging this self-talk through affirmations is a helpful approach that is highly recommended by both laypersons and mental health professionals.

Of course, when starting from a place of very low self-esteem, the typical "I am a strong and powerful warrior"-style affirmations can feel like a stretch. When you've struggled with a lifetime of getting bitch-slapped by your inner critic, the space between your self-concept and these empowered affirmations can feel like a massive chasm. Not to mention that the language for most mainstream affirmations feels pretty far off base for how many people usually think, feel, and speak. If your affirmations feel like too big of a stretch or if they use unrelatable, basic inspo-meme language, you probably won't be able to connect with them and be motivated to use them on a consistent basis. And if you *do* summon the fucks required to give it a go, you might just feel so ridiculous and disconnected that you won't get much from it.

As you've probably guessed, the feral self-care solution is to ditch the niceties and make this task unhinged! Part of what makes the human creature so unique is ingenuity. You are gifted with immense creativity and to lean into this is to find the secret sauce to help you heal your woes.

So craft unhinged affirmations that feel relatable and fun for you to use. This will be the secret to *actually using them* and having a little lighthearted fun in the process.

How to Do It

When crafting affirmations that will actually serve your self-care, lean into this creativity and dream up some of the most unhinged phrases you can. Don't worry about being polite or palatable; go full goblin mode and let yourself speak to yourself in...well, the way *you* speak.

Some ideas to get you started:

- I am strong and powerful, even when I feel like shit.
- I am a special and unique little chaos demon.
- I am worthy and valuable, like a collection of rare, haunted coins.
- I am like garlic in a recipe: Too much of me is still the right amount.
- I am a lovable, feral creature.

Roll out the cuss words, grab a dictionary for some medieval slang, or hell, even create some sort of poem or haiku! Do whatever works for you. The key is to just find the positives, have fun, and let loose.

Fail with Gusto!

In any creative or new endeavor, humans have a deep longing to succeed. "Success" (whatever that may mean for you) not only fulfills you as an individual, allowing you to take pride in your achievements, but as a social creature it also allows you to gain attention and social praise. Potent and intoxicating stuff!

Failure, on the other hand, is foolishly treated by members of the human species as something you should avoid at all costs. This is probably because failing requires you to navigate complex and painful emotions, such as shame, embarrassment, and rejection. (Those murky, icky feelings that you'd much rather leave stuffed in the basement of your awareness.) A good old-fashioned try followed by falling flat on your face can feel not only awful on a personal level but also downright catastrophic in the cases where other people get to witness it happen. This is likely why so many leave goals and aspirations unfulfilled, telling themselves that these dreams are "too unrealistic" to risk trying in the first place—a protective mechanism for avoiding the messy indignity of failure!

At the risk of sounding too morbid, you only have this one wild and surprising life! It should be spent living with gusto, not being restricted by the things that *might* go wrong. So what if you fail? The shame, embarrassment, guilt, and desire to cocoon forever are feelings that you likely play with anyway in the sprawling landscape of your mind, so why not bring them to life in a dizzying and courageous act of feral self-care? You can find yourself stripping away layers of fear and emerging as free by trying (and potentially failing) as loud as can be! In doing so, you both normalize the process of doing big, audacious things in the name of chasing our dreams and suck all the juicy, risky adventure from your limited time on this plane.

Embracing your messy humanity means accepting that not every experience has to feel good in order to be worthwhile. Shitty feelings aren't fun for sure, but in your efforts to avoid these states you can end up avoiding living itself. As an act of feral self-care, give yourself the loving permission to experience trying, failing, and everything in between!

Go forth and take those dreams, desires, and urges to create and let them fly free. And should you fail, then fail with gusto! Revel in the rush of doing the thing, outcome be damned. After all, failure is a spicy side effect of a life well lived!

How to Do It

Begin by thinking of something—just one simple thing to start—that you have always wanted to try that you've kept yourself from out of fear of failure.

Now *just go do that!* Do it shamelessly, with no regard for fear or "what ifs." Some examples could be:

- Taking an exercise class.
- Starting a business.
- Changing your hair or personal style.
- Initiating a book club or social circle.
- Taking up an ambitious art project.

Go forth and allow yourself to undertake something new with full permission to fail. This doesn't mean to *assume* you will fail. It just means to recognize that if you did fail, it really wouldn't be the end of the world. Fear of failure is like any other fear: Once you allow yourself to be exposed to it, it loses its power over you.

Allowing yourself to fail with gusto is a good sign you're living life right!

Create a Self-Care Playlist

As discussed earlier in this chapter, music is a powerful tool for the human creature. Through music you can time travel, engage in emotional cosplay, and get vibe checked into oblivion with just a few key notes and the tremble of words. All creative forms available to you are special; however, music is an art form that is as transcendent as it is versatile. There is a special place in the human heart for music, and the appreciation of it can be just as powerful as the creation of it itself.

Music has the ability to help you energetically and emotionally shape-shift. The vibration and energetics of sound are such that it is possible for the human creature to change in mood by simply listening to music. Some songs can move you to tears, while others can give you the strong urge to get up out of your seat and wildly bop around. All songs are medicine in their own right, and to understand the mechanism by which this art form affects you personally can act as a key to "hack" your own moods.

So get some creative feral self-care by making a special mixtape as an act of loving kindness to yourself! Using your knowledge of yourself and what things you like, what moves you, and what makes you feel deeply, give yourself the loving gift of a personalized self-care playlist that can bring you healing and joy again and again.

How to Do It

With programs that hold masses of music and the ability to arrange and rearrange song lists, making a playlist/mixtape is easier than ever. That being said, as an act of feral self-care, it's important to still give yourself the courtesy of carefully choosing the things that will be powerful and meaningful for you. Make your playlist(s) with intention.

Options for self-care playlists include:

- A master playlist, full of music that you like, that just *feels good* to listen to.
- Playlists that correspond to different "moods."
- Playlists that correspond to different self-care activities (e.g., "Mandi's Crying List").
- Playlists that correspond with the moods or vibes that you *want* to be in (e.g., a fun or cheerful mix for when you are feeling anything but).

The possibilities are endless. Does anything in particular come to mind when reading these examples?

The truly important thing is to undertake this in the spirit of love and care. Send that warm, loving energy from you to *you*!

Indulge In Your Comfort Arts

When you look at the chaotic unpredictability of being a person, it's no wonder that it's human nature to turn to familiar things to soothe and calm yourself. Life is full of variables that are completely beyond your control, and in times of turmoil and struggle, the stability and predictability of what is comforting can be medicine to soothe the frazzled soul. When you are feeling overwhelmed and adrift, it can be a powerful form of self-care to seek out the soothing presence of things you know and love.

Your "comfort arts" are the things that consistently bring you joy over time. These are the songs you play on repeat, the movies you've watched a thousand times, the artistic creations that are wholly and completely familiar to you. Turning to these things in times of struggle can feel like sinking into a warm bath or cuddling up in a thick, cozy blanket. Nothing unpredictable, no nasty surprises—just the pure, soothing experience of something you know and love well.

Is it nice to watch something new, challenge yourself, or branch out to satisfy that very human desire for novelty? Sure, but it's indisputable that sometimes you just want to dive into the comfort of something that is known, familiar, and safe. It doesn't matter what the genre the comfort art is, whether it makes you have an unhinged, soulful laugh or a deeply restorative cry: The important thing is that it is something deeply familiar and comforting for you. It soothes the soul like a warm, soft blankie.

Life can be hard at times, requiring a lot of your brain, your resilience, and your tired nervous system. The tried, tested, and true things allow you to mentally "check out," finding security and predictable, pleasant emotion in the things you can control. Intentionally turn to these arts as an act of feral self-care.

How to Do It

Chances are you likely already turn to the arms of your comfort arts automatically as a form of self-care when hitting a rough patch, but the intention of the following activity is to do so deliberately.

1. Make a list of the TV shows, movies, songs, etc. that you turn to again and again for mindless and predictable comfort throughout time. The purpose of the list is to have a clear tool kit for things to turn to when you're having a hard time, minimizing the amount of mental energy you'd have to spend trying to choose something to focus on.

2. To ramp up the fun (and the drama!) you could even keep this list on tiny scraps of paper housed in a Mason jar with a label that reads "Break in case of emergency!" to dig into when times are tough.

3. Choose which of these comfort arts you want to indulge in now. Is it a certain song? A specific episode of that beloved TV show? Maybe it's watching a cherished movie from your childhood. Whatever it is, take the time to lazily enjoy it, making it a fully relaxed, comfortable, cozy, and fulfilling experience.

Make Art from Authenticity

Feral self-care isn't just about vibing with nature and embracing what it is to be a human. It's also about the recognition that picture perfection isn't really something anyone should be aspiring to. Going feral in large part is recognizing that you are just right *exactly as you are* in all your messy, chaotic glory! Should you desire to shift and change and grow, you are the one who gets to direct the evolution, and it should be done in the spirit of authenticity rather than try to fit some bullshit ideals. When you begin to "find yourself," it typically *does* require change—changing in a manner that is more aligned with who you *truly* are.

Unleashing your authenticity is a gentle unfolding. An exfoliation of all the programming and conditioning that makes you feel as if you are unsafe in stepping up to who you really are. It is a rediscovering process—one where you reject the ideas of what you *should* and *could* become and instead seek to be authentically and radically free.

While this quest might sound exhilarating (which it is), it can also stretch you in ways that can feel frightening or uncomfortable. Part of the paradoxical experience of being human is the desire to be liberated as who you truly are while finding the lived experience of doing so to be simultaneously challenging. Luckily, as a creative and artistic being (yes, *you*), you can make this transformation easier on yourself by approaching it through the artist's lens. Truly, *you* get to decide what picture of yourself and your life you create. You are both the art and the artist in the amazing work of making the brightest, most audacious version of yourself! By approaching your authenticity as a work of art (and yes, it is work), you make your personal growth a place where desire, creativity, and freedom can bloom! Find feral self-care by creating this vision then using it as a map to guide you in self-expression.

How to Do It

Take some time to think about who you really are. Who would you be if you had no neighbors, friends, or family to influence you? Who would you be without the baggage of your past? Who would you be if you faked your own death and started all over with a community of fresh eyes? How would that person look, think, feel, and behave?

To make this practice into art, begin with the aesthetics of self-expression. Maybe it's doing your makeup differently. Or your hair. Maybe it's posing naked. Maybe it's covering yourself in body paint and screaming. In the privacy of your own home and your own life, take on the task of allowing yourself to practice this radical self-expression as an act of art.

If you want to be left with creative proof that will inspire you to fully unfold in this manner, feel free to do a little photo shoot, even if you don't share these pictures with *anyone*. And remember: Even the identity you play around with in this exercise may not be the final form. In every moment, you are a work in progress that is subject to creative change and evolution.

Be Eccentrically Sexy

This world is brimming with arbitrary, culturally imposed, and media-driven beauty standards that you can feel pressured to live up to. This utter bullshit has permeated most media spaces, but even worse, the deepest corners of the psyche. As a collective, people are bogged down with a crisis of confidence; every day you can turn on the TV or cruise the web and be faced with five hundred ways that you don't "measure up." There's an emphasis on appearances in society, and although you may know deep in your heart that substance is superior, it can be challenging not to fall into the trap of feeling "not good enough" in the realm of aesthetics and sex appeal.

This—like many things in modern society—is just an illusion. Is it true that those who fit conventional standards of "beauty" may be considered appealing to many people raised in this cultural context? Sure. But is that *all* there is to the kaleidoscopic, multidimensional nature of sexiness and attraction? Abso-fucking-lutely not! True sexiness is a *vibe* rather than an aesthetic. It's the feeling when you put on a certain color; it's the confidence that swells in your chest when you cope with something difficult in a strong and empowered way. Sexiness can look and be different things in different moments, and it doesn't rely on measuring up to any specific, culturally sanctioned ideals. *Period.*

With the rising incidence of depression, anxiety, self-loathing, etc. in modern society, it is imperative to take charge of shifting the narrative of what "sexy" is, recognizing the unique beauty and charisma that lies within every person as an individual. Whenever you sacrifice your mental health at the foot of rigid ideals, you miss out on uncovering what sexiness means for you personally and how your own one-of-a-kind, quirky, and embodied expression of sexiness helps empower you *and* pave the way for others to embrace their sexiness.

As an act of feral self-care, evict the generalized ideas of what it is to be sexy, and seek where this vibe is present for you in your own life and felt experience. Perhaps it is unshaved legs, dark-blue lipstick, and dancing wildly. Perhaps it's living your life to the fullest expression of your unhinged authenticity. Whatever it is, make sure it is *yours* so that you aren't measuring yourself up against something that you don't align with in the first place.

How to Do It

In order to tap into and express your own unique, eccentric sexiness, reflect on what feels authentically sexy for you. Depending on what you come up with, take the opportunity to play around a little with it. Some examples:

- Pick the outfit/hairstyle/makeup that unlocks this vibe and do a little photo shoot (don't worry, nobody has to see it).
- Use body or face paint on your skin.
- Make a list of situations or contexts where you feel the most sexy.
- Draw or paint a creative representation of your sexiness.
- Do some somatic bodywork, such as dancing or stretching while listening to music that unlocks a sexy vibe for you.
- Make a list of unusual things that you find sexy that do *not* fit the overall cultural ideals.

No matter what you do, the important thing is to realize that true sexiness, confidence, and allure is a vibe wholly unique to you. Any time spent stripping away the societal notions that take a cookie-cutter approach to what's "hot" is time well spent—and a truly important act of feral self-care.

Enjoy a Story

Storytelling has been a primal part of humanity throughout history. Prior to modernization, people used stories to explain the world around them, to transfer knowledge, and to entertain themselves. To communicate via stories, legends, and lore is such a fundamental part of being human, and fortunately the art of storytelling has endured the test of time. Even in the modern landscape, stories dominate awareness. They are what form the foundation of media and entertainment and the structure of conversations. And although modern culture dwells in the land of logic and reason, deep in our creature hearts, we are still suckers for a good story—the more far-fetched, emotionally gripping, hilarious, or mysterious the better! Stories are a place where human processing and creativity become entwined.

You may notice that the most enduring stories follow a certain structure or story arc. Stories of redemption, of overcoming hardship, of characters going through a series of challenges that induce some core transformation. These are the archetypal bones of the stories humans are drawn to, and in many cases, despite the distinct variation between the stories themselves, these narrative arcs are important. They speak to human values. In many cases, they speak to fears and desires. They may teach you something or surprise you by tugging at your emotions in meaningful ways. To indulge in a story is no idle task; it is meaningful, important, and deeply fulfilling on a human level.

So unabashedly enjoy a good story as an act of self-care. Allow yourself to become lost and swept up in it, and enjoy doing so as a primal gift of enjoyment for yourself. However, be aware of which stories you're indulging in. For best results, find an uplifting or nostalgic, pleasurable story and enjoy the ride! The ability for a story to shift your energy is powerful, so use this knowledge wisely. Stories with a darker vibe have their place but aren't necessarily the ones you dip into as a self-care strategy.

How to Do It

Approach this task as one that has just as high importance and priority as you'd approach essential tasks, such as doing work, washing the floors, or taking a shower. If you're the type who struggles with focus, motivation, or attention, doing this paired with things like housework and personal care (walking, bathing, and the like) can help you stay focused.

To begin, find a story to sink into. Perhaps it's a book, or maybe it's an audiobook, podcast, or maybe the opportunity to shoot the shit with a real person who is gifted in the art of storytelling (friends like this are true treasures)! Perhaps it is you who is both the storyteller *and* the story enjoyer!

If you are doing this alone with a podcast, audiobook, or something similar, block out a specific amount of time for this task. Enjoy it, and let it carry you away. If you're enjoying stories in a social setting, just simply go with the flow! When you're done, take a moment to appreciate how good it feels to give yourself this primal pleasure.

To push yourself further, ask yourself: "Do I have any stories that need telling?"

CHAPTER 5

NAVIGATING YOUR INNER DEPTHS

In order to truly connect with your authentic and feral nature, you must learn to navigate the swamp within yourself. As a human, you have many layers and murky depths. And your capacity for emotions and complex thinking can lead you to resist diving into these dark waters. It makes sense: They can seem pretty scary sometimes. However, some of the greatest things can happen when you dive in and root around that inner swamp.

When you allow yourself to journey inward, you learn fundamental truths about who you are, giving yourself the tools you need to show up authentically and wholly. The dark and scary corners of your awareness—the places where you store your traumas, insecurities, and negative tendencies—are where you can truly understand yourself, heal and grow, and find radical acceptance of all parts of your messy humanity! This chapter is all about diving into your own inner swamp. In these practices, you will find feral self-care in the tangled business of inner healing and accepting all the beauty *and* ugliness that lies within.

Take an "Ugly Day"

The modern world has its priorities all backward. There's an overall sense that productivity is worth, appearances are truth, and fitting in is the only acceptable way to live.

This is pure bullshit! You are not always meant to be productive, palatable, and to have it all figured out. Sometimes you are meant to wallow, process your emotions, and let yourself sit with the ugliness of what you feel.

An ugly day is a mental health day where you shamelessly and unapologetically allow yourself to wallow in the filth of your own struggle. This means giving yourself full permission to be honest about your feelings, look as bad as you feel, and behave in a way that is in no way civilized or polite. Wallow you shall! In a society that's normalized putting on a show and going through the motions to keep up your income, social standing, and even self-concept, taking an ugly day is a radical act of self-care.

So what if you look like you rolled out of a ditch? So what if you don't tackle a thing on that to-do list? So what if you feel more rabid racoon than human and are in no fit condition to be social at all?

So. What.

To honor the very human need you have to process your emotions rather than stuff them down is to give yourself a gift. You are giving yourself the space and opportunity to sit with the hard stuff and pave the way for the good that's sure to come. Obligations and appearances be damned!

So gift yourself the opportunity of a mental health day that gives zero fucks.

How to Do It

Take a full day to yourself to wallow as a form of valid healing. Play hooky from whatever obligations you have, turn your phone on "do not disturb," make sure your comfort foods are stocked, and close the damn curtains so the neighbors can't witness your spiral. Your uniform? Maybe it's a messy bun and pajamas. Maybe it's a dinosaur onesie. You do you! This is your time to be as ugly and slobby as you please.

Spend your ugly day doing whatever feel-good things strike in the moment. Watch ridiculous movies, listen to hours of *High Strangeness* podcasts, paint, or simply just zone out on your couch. Many of the activities in this very book can be tackled on your ugly day! The important thing is that it's all about you, baby—and there is no obligation to look, feel, or act a certain way. This is a day that exists outside the usual pressures of being a human. A day you can be more goblin than person!

When the feelings come knocking (and they will come knocking!), take the day to let yourself sit with them and just allow them to be. You have nobody to impress and nothing to achieve at this moment. Nothing but nonjudgmentally letting yourself feel all the things so that tomorrow you might feel a little lighter.

Rage Clean

In keeping with the ethos of feral self-care, it's important that you allow for the *full* spectrum of human emotion. Part of liberating your authentic self is being emotionally honest and not bypassing or squashing down the shitty feelings in an attempt to pretend everything is okay. Because truthfully, sometimes things are decidedly *not* okay! To go feral is to acknowledge, and even (gasp!) embrace, that fact.

A fun way to deal with the bad feelings is to approach them in the spirit of play. While you can't *always* do this (sometimes it just hurts too much), the option is often there to clown around with the concept of unapologetically wallowing in whatever nasty, grimy thing you're feeling. This is particularly true when it comes to anger. On occasion, while you are alone, it can be fun to lean way into the kind of petty, foot-stomping, petulant vibe that is typically not encouraged in polite society. Have some feral fun with some feral feelings! A great way to do this is to indulge in a little rage cleaning. It's a fun, unhinged way to blow off steam.

Rage cleaning is, well, all the rage (ha!) because it allows you to channel your anger into something positive and productive. Just be cautious with the breakables! There's a high likelihood you've done this intuitively in your life when dealing with stress, anxiety, or while trying to distract yourself from the toxic urge to exact some revenge. Rage cleaning can be therapeutic and emotionally affirming, with the side effect of leaving you with a sparkly clean space. It's truly a win-win all around!

So the next time you're feeling some type of way, take all that icky, negative emotion and turn it into fuel for a little tidy up! It's a wonderfully deranged way of saying "fuck you" to the concept of burying your emotions and a fantastic tool for feeling your feelings. As a method of feral self-care, you will likely find it to be a useful way to both process emotion *and* honor the messy spectrum of the human experience—yes, even the negative aspects.

How to Do It

The next time you're feeling angry or upset and fighting the urge to crawl out of your skin or go key someone's car (not recommended!), turn on some aggressive music, such as techno or metal—anything else that gets the blood pumping. Then begin to clean your house or tidy up a pile of stuff you've been putting off for a while.

To really get unhinged, feel free to make this as dramatic a display of emotion as you can muster. If sorting clothing, literally throw the items to where they belong! If washing surfaces, scrub that bitch like you're cleaning a crime scene! This pairs well with other feral self-care activities, such as primal screaming and getting rid of unneeded items.

By cleansing your home in this state, you are also cleansing your emotional state—taking the time to channel all that energy into something that will serve you better.

Lean Into Lazy

Productivity culture is the vibe killer of the modern Western world. Humans need adventure, purpose, play, and rest! Sadly, with domestication, priorities are all messed up, and it can often feel like any time not spent doing something "important," "lucrative," or "purposeful" is not only time wasted but also morally reprehensible and totally irresponsible!

However, the truth is that sometimes you just need to allow yourself to be completely and unashamedly lazy. No plans, no purpose. Just general loitering and lollygagging and accomplishing nothing!

It's called self-care, baby!

In a feral sense, your ancestors didn't have the luxury to be lazy whenever they wanted. Survival was the name of the game, and throughout history this was the focus (or else!). However, did this mean people didn't need rest and the medicine of aimlessness? Not at all. Even in nature documentaries you can see that other animals cycle through periods of activity and simply lounging around. It's fundamental in the sense of conservation of energy. Basically, if you laze around when you can, you'll have more gas in the tank to run or be resourceful when the necessity comes.

What's the point of living in the modern world with all its convenience and survival needs checked off if not to enjoy the luxuries it provides? You *can* be lazy and still survive. You *can* lounge and lollygag and loiter; your chances of being eaten by a tiger will still probably be quite low. From a primal mammalian perspective, those are some great odds!

So push past the almighty worship of busy and look to being a lil' lazy and slobby as an act of tender feral self-care. Take a break for fuck's sake; your problems will still be there tomorrow!

How to Do It

Allowing yourself to be deliberately and intentionally lazy only works as valid self-care when planned correctly. For example, if you have a big project or deadline due, chances are leaning into lazy is not going to *feel* supportive, and you won't get the most bang for your buck.

But when you *can* afford to be lazy, shamelessly allow yourself to do so. If you're the type who struggles to do this guilt-free and can't turn your brain off, then make a list of reasons why doing this is an appropriate and beneficial act. For example:

- If I'm lazy now, I will have more energy to work later.
- If I'm lazy now, I am feeding future creativity.
- If I'm lazy now, I'll be less likely to want to throw hands when people bug me.
- If I'm lazy now, I'll be more rested to fistfight the tides of circumstances later.

However you need to justify it to yourself, do that. *But*, more importantly, let yourself realize (and don't you dare forget it!) that sometimes doing *less* is self-care that not only helps you but also shifts the way you move through the world. It's an act of love that ripples not only through your own life but has the potential to heal others.

Honor Your Seasons

As discussed in Chapter 2, part of living feral is to work with the seasons and cycles of nature. However, you have your *own* seasons as well. These are the various highs and lows you face throughout your life in any given year. These cycles may not necessarily sync up with those in nature; however, they may still reflect the vibe of cycles in nature. For example, times of wintery rest, times of free summer joy, and times of new beginnings reflecting the fresh energy of spring. Although there are those who align quite well with the seasonal energies of the regions where they live, others may find themselves coming alive in winter and hibernating in summer, for example!

Modern civilization ticks on regardless of the seasons or even your own internal needs for play or rest, so it is up to *you* to connect with self-understanding and honor these cycles so you can avoid burning yourself to the ground. This kind of self-knowledge can help you immensely in not pushing yourself too hard and honoring your own unique timelines.

As a conscious being, you are influenced by the experiences that have shaped you. On a cyclical basis, there may be times you become overcome with grief coinciding with some past event. Or patterns where your energy will naturally swell and wane as with any other resource. You have completely unique cycles and timelines that come together to form your individualized "calendar" system, consisting of your celebrations, grief, lulls, bursts of energy, and so on. In knowing these cycles, you can give yourself the loving space to cope and thrive.

The modern world demands you to take a cookie-cutter approach to living. You are expected to press on throughout the year, with little to no regard for how your natural inclinations or cycles flow. Find feral self-care by learning what your natural "seasons" are, making room for the expression of these seasons so they work to your advantage.

How to Do It

Reflect on what your unique cycles and rhythms are. Maybe you hate summer and find yourself with more energy and creativity in the fall. Maybe you spend every spring wracked by grief. Whatever it is, it doesn't need to make any sense to anyone except you. What you're looking to investigate is how your energy and mood shift throughout the year in positive, negative, and neutral ways. Take all this information and use it to create your own customized "calendar" for the year. Take note of specific celebratory or triggering dates, months, seasons, and occurrences.

If you're struggling to sort out what your seasons are, then you can start by doing some mood and energy tracking. Commit to doing so for a year. As the next year rolls around, make note of any similarities or recurring patterns. These form the basis of your unique seasons, and although they will shift and evolve over time, it's still valuable information to have.

Burrow Into Grief

Humans by nature are deeply emotional creatures. You have the capacity for a wide range of feelings, but sadly, only the "good" ones seem to be socially acceptable to express openly. Despite the supportive memes and folks paying lip service to "feel your feelings," many people still limit themselves from sharing the multidimensional range of *all* points on the raw emotional spectrum.

One emotion that's particularly uncomfortable is grief. Although everyone has been touched by grief in some way throughout life, it's one of those tricky, shape-shifting states that can confuse and disturb both the person experiencing it and those who witness it. Grief is typically defined as an intense feeling of sorrow, but even this definition doesn't do it justice. Grief is an emotion that knows no time boundaries or logic, and it's one that can be triggered by a variety of circumstances across the lifespan.

The modern world simply isn't set up for people to grieve with the kind of loving space that is required when holding something so heavy. You are still required to work, fulfill obligations, pay bills, and continue caregiving despite living through this monstrous experience. Unlike your ancestors, you likely don't live in a small community that is built around mutual support for one another and the space to heal through grief. And what's worse is that many have lost touch with grief to the point of holding both internal and external ideas of how long it "should last" and when it's "appropriate" to be felt.

Sometimes the best thing is to fully burrow into your grief, to honor the complexity of this emotion without placing undue expectations upon yourself. Sometimes the most healing thing is to lean way into the felt experience of grief, giving it a place to settle in so you can process it better. As a society and as a community of people who all have the capacity to feel its chasmic depths, everyone needs to treat it with love and understanding. Allow yourself to drop the urge to fight it in favor of letting it take up space (because it will whether you consciously allow it or not).

So make way for the enormity of grief as a valid form of feral self-care. Give yourself the gift of a cry and space to grieve. It's okay to howl at the moon in despair. It's okay to allow your tears to mingle with the watery ocean. It's okay to burrow into your grief for a spell, letting yourself fully experience the dreadful wretchedness of it.

How to Do It

When you are feeling deep in grief, let it wash over you without self-judgment or putting a time limit on its presence. Allow the tears to flow, and channel the pain through your body with movement and/or primal screams and howls. Give not one single fuck what you look like or what you sound like. Simply allow the raw emotion to move through you with love, self-compassion, and grace.

To further boost the benefits, surround yourself with a community of people who will hold space for your grief and all sides of your emotional expression. Give freely the kind of love and support you wish to receive. Be emotionally honest, which in turn will normalize the experience and expression of difficult feelings. Be a safe space for yourself and for others.

Brawl with Your Inner Critic

Ahhh, the inner critic. That overbearing, taunting asshole that lives inside your head, making you feel chronically devalued and imposterish. Since this inner critic lives in the intimate file room that is your mind, it knows *exactly* what to whisper to you in order to mess with your flow.

It's time to show that bitch who's boss!

Although it may sound counterintuitive, sometimes the best thing to do is to pass that noisy devil the mic. This may mean getting yourself comfortable with a little incense, candles, comforting music and scents, maybe a little dressed up so you feel fabulous, and then writing out *loudly* all the things that your inner critic is trying to whisper in your ear. After all, the inner critic can act like a toddler having a tantrum: Ignoring it won't necessarily make it go away. In fact, you may find it gets emboldened and louder.

"You're a failure!"

"Everyone hates you!"

"The whole world is going to find out you're an idiot!"

Write it all out. In detail. The more ridiculous the better. Does your critic want you to think you're annoying? The least favorite neighbor? That you smell like Parmesan cheese? Write. All. That. Dumb. Stuff. Down.

As a form of unhinged feral self-care, this method is fun and effective. Indulging your inner critic to have their say can feel deliciously hysterical when you read this back in excruciating detail, marveling in how completely unhinged it is.

The avoidance of feeling bad can lead you to more discomfort than that you are trying to avoid. When you get it all out on the table, that's when you reclaim your power and can begin to challenge the shadows that give that stuff credence in the first place. For example, some of it will be obvious and easy to challenge: The most annoying person ever? Come on, you can think of ten more annoying people you've encountered in a single day running errands! Others may give valuable insight on things inside that are screaming for healing.

As for the smackdown: Well, there is a lot of feral self-care to be found in not only giving the inner critic an audience but actively fighting back!

How to Do It

1. Make your list of everything your inner critic is saying.
2. Read how obscenely ridiculous this list is, and revel in the unhinged nature of your inner critic.

Now it's time to brawl: Pick up your list, take a few deep breaths, then rip it up or safely burn it while stating newer, better ideas about yourself aloud. Speak them into fruition. This is how you release, banish, and take the power back from that inner bully.

Of course, there are other ways you can complete this "fight," including:

- Putting the list onto a chair and talking shit back at it.
- Burying the list and planting something on top of it to show that you will use that nonsense for growth.
- Ripping up the list and then using the strips for papier-mâché art.
- Mounting the list outside and screaming at it while throwing old tomatoes and such at it.

The possibilities are truly endless. Just make sure that it's fun! At the end of the day what you are trying to do here is give the inner critic a voice so you can expose how asinine it is, then reclaim your power by fighting back.

Kiss Some of These Cares Goodbye

Chances are right now at this very moment you, dear human, are giving way too many fucks about *something* in your life.

That is to say there are things that you are carrying that are taking up valuable space in your head and in your heart—things that deserve to be set down. As human beings, our ability to care, to plan, and to think are wonderful assets, but the cursed side effects of that are that we sometimes take on the load of far more than we can handle, messing up our vibe and energy in the process.

At any given point you are likely juggling an invisible load that's weighing you down even more than you may be aware of. As you move through this shit show of being a person, you accumulate all these things you're supposed to care about all the time: what other people will think of you, how you are going to be received, stress about people you care for, worries about controlling XYZ....You end up with this massive load of mental, emotional, and energetic debris that can be hard to shake or put down. Even the things you've outgrown or potentially thought you've healed, such as worries about an ex or a friend you've cut ties with, can linger still, and it can take a considerable amount of work to consciously disconnect from all that stuff.

When it comes to anxieties, we can carry deep, almost superstitious, fears about letting them go. Although there are a variety of reasons for this, ultimately it can leave us with a feeling of doom or a sense that we are dropping the ball or doing something "bad" by putting these things down. But, my dear feral friend, you are not required to lift these things in perpetuity. As you grow and shift and evolve, so too should the load you carry. Although it can feel like dropping the ball, the truth is that some balls are meant to be dropped, or better: thrown into the abyss completely! As a creature of the wild, you only have so much energy and mental space to deal with *all the things*—a little mental declutter could do you a world of good!

How to Do It

Similar to the Create a Shit List activity in Chapter 4, your task is to write down a list of cares (anxieties, worries, concerns, etc.) that you're ready to give up:

1. Take some paper and cut or tear it up into small scraps.
2. On each piece of paper, write a care that you want to let go of. With each item, it's worth considering how draining it is, how worrying about it inhibits other areas of life, and how it would feel to be relieved of it.
3. Then as an act of symbolic release that feeds into the primal spirit of feral self-care, literally kiss each scrap of paper (with lipstick as an added symbolic boost, if you choose) and then burn it, crumple it up and throw it in the trash, or rip it up into teensy-weensy pieces. Whatever you choose, the important thing is to affirm to yourself that you're giving this up—*in the spirit of wild and lighthearted fun*—to make space for greater and better cares.

Revel in the Absurdity of Life

Although there is no handbook for how to human, there are a few key lessons everyone ends up learning along the way. One of these key lessons is that despite all your planning and attempts to control everything, life is a space of unpredictable chaos. In any given lifetime, there are a variety of experiences that run the emotional gamut: There are happy times, hard times, and things that occur that are so completely batshit crazy you just *have* to laugh so you don't cry yourself off the rails.

Weaving chaos is a fundamental aspect of feral self-care. It is the acknowledgment that despite all your best-laid plans, you are ultimately at the mercy of a million variables that you could never fully imagine. Life is inherently absurd, ridiculous, downright laughable in the sense that you can go around trying to batten down the hatches, preparing for all the things, but ultimately there is no planning in this Molotov cocktail of simply existing!

One of the best ways to train your resilience and learn to let go is to go all in looking for the humor in the absurdity of life. Because, darling, it's there whether you like it or not! Humor is healing, and even the simple act of acknowledging whatever disastrous mess you are in (regardless of the details) is a powerful act of surrender and feral self-care. Additionally, finding humor in stressful situations has wide-ranging physical and mental health benefits as well.

The ability to laugh in a crisis is literally good for your health! It helps your brain release feel-good chemicals and improves your ability to manage stress.

Whether it's reveling in the absurdity of your own mental tendencies, the circumstances of your life, or in the *audacity* of some people, typically the most healing and cathartic method of self-care is to shake your head and have a laugh. After all, those problems? They're still going to be there whether you like it or not. But in learning to find the humor, you humble yourself and find resilience, putting more pep in your step to tackle things with ease!

How to Do It

Although it can be hard to find the humor in life's deranged twists and turns, sometimes it can help to imagine your life as some sort of cosmic soap opera: a lil' something for the aliens to watch. A cinematic hot mess!

Think of some of the most insane things that you are dealing with, some of the more neurotic internal tendencies, or the utter ridiculousness of that recent hot streak of bad luck. As you think about these things, take a deep breath and try to gently find the humor. Although it may take some digging if you are truly in the thick of it, I promise there *is* humor there to be had (time and hindsight typically helps suss it out).

The important thing to remember is that although things might be completely next-level, bizarro insane, they have been so before and will be again. 'Tis part of both life and the human condition! Revel in the absurdity of it all, but most of all, be gentle as you move through this chaotic soup called life.

Take a Tech Fast

In the modern age, tech reigns king, and this progress has happened so fast that many can still remember a time when this wasn't the case. The level of technological advancements humans have made has been astronomical, and the truth is that it's done the species, and individual lives, a lot of good. We've all benefited in many ways from technological advances. Medical tech can be literally lifesaving, aiding in surgeries and improving quality of life. Other more mundane tech has helped us to enjoy comforts and conveniences that would dazzle our ancestors. However, there have also been some...growing pains along the way.

In the industrialized world, most are connected to a degree that would make their primal ancestors' heads spin. With social media and the Internet itself, you are only ever a swipe away from what feels like all the information in the world—from the minutiae of some random person's lunch choices to infinite libraries and catalogs of information on pretty much any given subject.

It's a roller coaster, baby.

As the "dominant" species on this planet, it can be easy to feel as if we are infallible. Like we can both cope with and overcome anything that comes our way. However, the truth is more complex: We are deeply emotional beings. Moved and affected by things in such a way that can be subtle yet all-consuming. And we have simply not evolved to handle this constant connectivity that characterizes life today. This constant connection, although beneficial in some respects, seemed to sneak up on the world, and the results are not all good for the human species or our relationship to our wild. It's become a symbol of domesticity and of the severed tie many have both to nature and to themselves.

A feral necessity, not to mention an incredibly potent form of self-care, is to take a break from this ever-present connection so you can sit once again with the quiet stillness of being alone. Accompanied only by your thoughts and by your intuition. So take a tech fast as a way to nurture your wild and to get acquainted once again with the comforting stillness of being alone.

How to Do It

Set aside some time each day to be completely disconnected. This can be done at your home or even while out doing something, such as hiking or spending time outdoors. This isn't just about blocking out the Internet, news, and tech itself. This is also about spending some time unreachable by other people, as chances are you have become accustomed to getting immediate responses and being able to reach people at any given time at the expense of your ability to be perfectly, serenely alone.

Give yourself the gift of pure silence and disconnection. Humans need some alone time. You require space from the constant connection and stimulation that has become so normalized for you. This is important not only for your mental health but for your connection with yourself.

Seek Out Discipline

No discussion of self-care would be complete without a little tough love. Although self-care strategies to some extent rely on a model of grace giving and radical acceptance of where you're at, there needs to be some balance. Discipline can be a triggering word, especially for those who have none and live like unpredictable, chaotic little gremlins. However, the truth is that everyone needs to have *some* of it in order to get best results in the arena of self-care.

The ability to have discipline has done the human species a lot of good. The tendency to work hard and make things happen deliberately and with thoughtful attention has helped people survive throughout the ages. However, the way things are set up in modernity doesn't require so much of you in the survival sense. Many cultures are now steeped in a vibe of instant gratification (the ability to get what we want fast without considering the potential consequences of such). Many people struggle with discipline when they may not have learned to cultivate it in the first place. Still, humans have a primal need for discipline in order to thrive, and it can be a rare and precious thing in the modern landscape.

To cultivate self-discipline is something that can enhance many areas of life far beyond simply self-care. Although "meeting yourself where you're at," being gentle with yourself, and not beating yourself up are all extremely important for your experience of life, sometimes what you actually *need* more than anything is a little ass kicking. From a gentle kick in the pants to a stern "get your shit together," discipline is a gift only *you* can give *yourself*! This is what moves people to improve our circumstances and to go about doing things in a thoughtful and effective way.

So as a great way to exploit your natural human abilities, seek discipline in your life as an avenue for feral self-care. Because the cold, hard facts are that self-care is not only about doing the things that *feel* good. Sometimes it's about doing things you hate that are ultimately for your best interests. Sometimes it's about doing things that you kind of suck at. Sometimes it's about creating structure so you can thrive.

How to Do It

Pick one single goal that would be the most impactful and inspiring for you to achieve and commit to prioritizing that goal for the next three weeks. Now, it's important to do this in a disciplined yet *kind* way. Contrary to what your brain may think, it isn't actually all that motivating to bully yourself into submission. And expectations that rely on perfection with no room for the ebbs and flows of your own energy and motivation are similarly destined to fail.

Set yourself some clearly defined steps for tackling this goal you've chosen. Even go further by creating a ritual or routine that will make approaching this easier. For example, make your disciplined actions into a game or some sort of vibey experience. You're ultimately more motivated to do things when they don't feel like a drag.

Which leads into the final point: It may be worth exploring your mindset on the topic of discipline. Is this a topic that brings up some old wounds? Does it bring up feelings of inadequacy? Are there mucky feelings of shame? Does the word itself make you want to strip naked and run into a field? Ultimately, self-knowledge and understanding can help you begin to reframe concepts like discipline so that we see them as a loving gift you give yourself rather than a punishment or chore.

Make Some Space

As discussed earlier in this book, the modern world is loaded with *stuff*. As a consumerist culture, there's a solution sold for every problem, and people accumulate masses of things they *think* they need, when in reality the practical needs of humans are actually pretty basic. Food, water, love, and a few other things that won't necessarily take up space on a shelf are all you need.

Your early ancestors were frequently on the move for survival, with few opportunities to gather and accumulate masses of stuff. But now many can sit comfortably in houses and order almost anything they like from all over the world with just the press of a button. Leaving only the problem of paying the bill and figuring out where to put it all! An interesting shift for the species' development for sure.

However, just because you *can* get all of this stuff doesn't mean you *should*. Sometimes this accumulation of things can come with a lot of mental baggage. And you can find some feral self-care in "cleaning house," or getting rid of things that are just sitting around taking up space.

Although getting rid of your old junk and treasures may not sound like self-care, the truth is that often your spaces reflect what you are feeling inside. And when your spaces become too overrun with stuff, much like your mind, they could benefit from a lil' tidy. A physical and energetic ritual of symbolic *and* practical release!

As many who advocate for the minimalist craze will tell you, sometimes this accumulation of stuff can end up feeling heavier than we realize. In getting rid of things that are just taking up space, even just on the fringes of your awareness, you are left to better appreciate the things you have—or the things you should be focusing on that take up no space at all, like the love in your life, the joys you experience, and the relationships that are so important to you.

There is nothing bad or wrong about collecting, wanting, or having things. But sometimes, you can find some liberation in being very intentional about what you choose to have and what you choose to release; both can be self-care. Sometimes in letting things go, you free up both physical and mental space for other better things to come.

How to Do It

Take some time to clean house. And by "clean house," I mean: Get. Rid. Of. Some. Shit!

If there are things you're holding on to that are making you feel bad (such as your "skinny pants," or items for hobbies that you feel bad about abandoning), start with those. You always have the ability to get new things later, but the mental "load off" that may come with the release now might just be priceless.

Alternatively, the task of making space can be approached in a more "backward" way. Look at the things you *do* have and consider which are things you love that bring you happiness and enhance your life. Intentionally and deliberately keep those things, and keep asking yourself the question "What is this bringing to my life?" as a litmus test for whether to keep other stuff.

Align to Your Daily Cycles

Throughout this book, you've explored the importance of cycles—not just the cycles of nature but your own internal cycles. And while some of those cycles are spread across time and seasons, you also have shorter-term, daily cycles that affect how you show up and feel on any given day.

Modern adulthood finds many people stuffed into routines that don't really suit their true nature. The problem with this is that you can spend a lot of your energy fighting uphill battles resisting the flow of your internal rhythms. In society as it stands now, the cycles of the individual are not typically considered. How could they be? With so many humans all having their own unique rhythms, it would be impossible to set things up to cater to everybody. You also have to factor in the natural cycle of the day (when it is light versus dark).

However, although there are valid reasons for the fact that the average person's life is structured fairly similarly in terms of when they work, play, and rest, that doesn't mean that this is necessarily supportive. Luckily, even though you might still be stuck on "the man's clock" rather than your own, you can still help yourself by learning what your own cycles are throughout the day. This info can be helpful for you, as there are surely sneaky little ways you can restructure your days and obligations so that you aren't constantly fighting with yourself every step of the way. Tackling this is likely to bring exponentially more self-care benefits than any bath bomb could ever dream of!

So take some time to discover your daily cycles as a matter of interest and a method to find your flow. Too much of life is spent trying to force yourself to fit into some cookie-cutter model; find some feral self-care by liberating yourself in any small ways you can!

How to Do It

If you are aware of your energy and mood cycles through the day already, then congratulations! You're actually ahead! If not, there are a few things to begin to take note of and track in order to get a better sense of your cycles. These include:

- When you feel the most creative.
- "Slumps" or times when you feel sleepy.
- "Bursts" or when you feel energy.
- Moods throughout the day (when you feel content, annoyed, etc.).
- When you feel clearheaded or motivated.

If you begin to keep track of these in a journal or diary, you can find helpful information that you can use to structure the parts of your life you *do* have control over. For example, if you notice your energy dips after meals, you can focus on tackling projects that require you to have more steam *before* eating. Or if you discover that your most creative time is at night, you might want to work on your art projects in the evening rather than try to force things when you won't be in a state of flow.

One thing to keep in mind as you approach this endeavor is that as a unique and ever-evolving individual, what you learn may be subject to change. It is totally normal for your cycles to shift and change over time, just as human beings are constantly shifting and changing! If you feel as if you have "outgrown" your cycles as you've gotten to know them, feel free to revisit this activity and make note of any changes.

Make Peace with Naked

Although everyone is born naked and howling like their primate relatives, as people age and develop, they trade in feral nudity for the cover of clothing. The use of clothing has allowed humans to thrive and be comfortable, as it can protect from the elements, keep in warmth, and provide a barrier to protect the skin.

Although clothing is undoubtedly beneficial, there are also benefits to be had in embracing your body in its natural, nude form. I'm talking getting naked, stripping to your birthday suit, doing the full Monty! The self-care benefits you can get from taking the time to heal your relationship with the wildness of your body and to become comfortable with nudity blow any spa day right out of the water! Spending more time naked can help people find significant improvements in self-esteem, body image, and comfort with themselves, just to name a few.

But what's a feral creature to do when they struggle to make peace with their meat suit? Although it would be wonderful if everyone could all appreciate their worldly vessels in all their natural glory, the truth is that for many, nudity brings up difficult feelings that may include guilt, shame, and insecurity.

Although there can be a variety of personal reasons for this discomfort, including trauma or negative experiences, modern humans as a whole are influenced to be uncomfortable with nudity in many cultures. All around you are subtle and not-so-subtle messages that condemn or place puritanical values upon your body, not to mention the shaming and culturally imposed beauty ideals that wriggle into your awareness and can make even your most private moments fraught with self-consciousness.

It's wild how something so natural can be such a fucking mess!

While it may not be fun at first, cultivate a loving acceptance of your birthday suit as a form of feral self-care. Return to a feeling of safety and acceptance toward your most primal and natural state—being a naked animal creature of the earth!

How to Do It

Making peace with your nudity has a couple of components, firstly mindset. You need to examine your ideas (both cultural and personal) toward nudity. This includes beauty ideals, how safe you feel being naked, how you conceptualize modesty and sexuality in respect to nakedness, and how you feel in your animal body when you are nude. Phew, that's a whole mixed bag of stuff! However, this mindset piece is crucial, as the way you as a human interpret the world and also your own self-concept are rooted in your beliefs about yourself.

The next component is exposure. To get comfortable with your own nudity, particularly if you're a person who struggles with body image, it can be really helpful to spend some time totally naked in private. Give yourself a safe space to begin accepting your body. At first this will feel very uncomfortable and may make every cell in your body scream "WTF," but persist! Build up to viewing your body in the mirror and becoming comfortable and safe with what you see. All the jiggly bits, marks, and imperfections—every single thing that is your pure, natural form. Stare at it till you love it! Let soft, cozy blankets slip over your skin! Touch kindly all the parts of you that you have not yet made peace with!

In your most feral state, you are naked just as you were born. This primal body is not a place to store shame and comparisons. It is your home and the vehicle through which you get to experience this one wild and beautiful life!

Embrace Discomfort

One of the most life-changing things contemporary humans can do is to learn to embrace discomfort. You've probably heard the quotes about amazing things existing on the other side of fear, but beyond that you need to *truly* understand the following: Your life can only become wonderfully expansive in proportion to how much discomfort you are willing to tolerate.

Modern human life is steeped with comfort. We're comfortable in our temperature-controlled homes. We're comfortable in our structured societies. We're even comfortable in the ruts of our daily routines! Human domestication, while not necessarily always pleasant, is certainly characterized by comforts both big and small. There is truly something around every corner to soothe and distract from the ever-present boogeyman that is the unknown.

However, the more you are willing to experience discomfort, the further you are capable of going. Many of the things you fear, from setting boundaries with a loved one all the way to pursuing the biggest dream, are quite doable. As emotional creatures of habit that crave safety, we hold ourselves off from things out of the desire to avoid feeling uncomfortable. But it's this avoidance that is at the root of most feelings of being "stuck."

The truth is that if you allowed yourself to stand bravely in the experience of discomfort, you would be able to tackle most of the things that are in the way of your best life. In many cases it would only take a brief while of pushing through this feeling of discomfort to do a world of good. That discomfort you can spend a lifetime avoiding may only be ten minutes of agony in practice. It is in the imagination space, that realm of amplifying anxiety, that it becomes a monster that's larger than life.

So return to your wild as a creature of the chaotic and expansive unknown by increasing your tolerance of that which feels uncomfortable. Doing so will have you equipped to handle most of what life throws at you with grace and ease. The impossible will feel at your fingertips, and you will establish yourself as the boss!

How to Do It

Jump on every juicy opportunity to get comfortable with discomfort as it comes! This means recognizing when you feel deeply uncomfortable or anxious, recognizing when you long to control the situation, and then just sitting with those raw feelings until the panic subsides. Hold the line! Deliberately feel into discomfort without fleeing the situation or trying to "make things better."

For added feral self-care benefits, practice *deliberately* putting yourself in situations that are unquestionably uncomfortable but also ripe with rewards. When you allow yourself to do this and follow through, you stretch yourself in ways that are gloriously awful *and* freeing! You show yourself that you are in charge of your growth and your healing. And you *will* find liberation and growth along the way.

Open Up Your Self-Concept

We humans are born as wild, feral little creatures. Then as we move along through life, we begin to collect a series of beliefs and "truths" that we fold into our understanding of who we are. This ultimately becomes the "script" that governs our lives. Your subconscious self-concept, or who it is you *believe yourself to be*, is the playbook that runs the show behind the scenes. These are the beliefs secretly calling all the shots, both limiting and motivating you.

The development of your self-concept is formed by your "programming": media influences, how your loved ones respond to you, your schooling, socialization, and the like. From childhood you absorb all this input telling you "who you are," forming a picture of yourself based on what you hear from those around you. You evaluate how you respond to others and how others respond to you and carefully craft a sense of self that feels comprehensive. However, this conditioning can be rigid and oppressive and may just be the thing holding you back.

The good news is that at any point *you* have the power to shift the narrative. Your self-concept is always in a state of flux, and you and you alone have the power to allow this constant alchemy to flow in a state of effortless ease. If the self-concept you've been carrying hasn't been supportive for your experience of life, you have the option to consciously create an updated "script." If there are things you don't like in your current script, you can tend to them. If there are things you love, you can feel grateful for them.

You decide!

Your feral self-care assignment is to recognize the incredible potential you have as a creator of your own life and story. "Who you are," whether it be prescribed to you by others or reinforced by years of self-talk, isn't law. It's malleable and dynamic in the face of new feelings, thoughts, and experiences.

Challenge your self-concept so you can quit bringing pilot-episode energy to the later seasons of your life!

How to Do It

To tidy up your self-concept, you must spend some time figuring out *what it exactly is*. Maybe you think of yourself as insecure. Maybe you think of yourself as too pushy. Maybe you consider yourself a pushover. With each thing you think to be a core truth about who you are, ask yourself: "Is this true because it's *actually* true or because I *believe* it to be?"

On a separate piece of paper, make two columns. Put your beliefs about who you are in the left column, and challenge each belief in the right column. Try and suss out whether you've been operating for too long with an outdated narrative that no longer fits.

Even in your most vulnerable moments, your power to shift the narrative and embrace the messy chaos of being unapologetically you is always at your fingertips. It just requires a little self-awareness and a willingness to dig deeply into the programming you have picked up over your lifetime.

Who *they said* you were no longer matters.

Who *you think* you are no longer matters.

You are the clay and the sculptor. You're the emotion that drives the hand, and the eyes that look on in wonder. You are the sauce. You are the magic!

Outsource Self-Love

In our messy humanity, often the biggest problems we face are caused by that hunk of meat that sits inside our pretty lil' skulls. As conscious beings, everything we go through in life is filtered through the subjective lens of our awareness. Add this to the absolute clusterfuck of messages that permeate the culture around us, stressing the fact that as we are is *never quite good enough*, and you have yourself a recipe for disaster when it comes to self-love!

Self-love isn't actually as simple as chanting affirmations and lazing around in a bathtub full of rose petals. Self-love is complex and even frightening, dredging up all sorts of raw and difficult feels from the murky depths of your swampy shadows. A journey toward self-love isn't only liberation and fuzzy feelings. And it's probably one of the most important things to tackle if you want to stabilize your entire life. After all, a person with a solid foundation of self-love will be way less likely to put up with bullshit, will prioritize their health and happiness, and will be willing to be uncomfortable sometimes for the greater good of their wellness.

But what if you're the type that's so far removed from self-love that you don't even know where to start? Such an unhinged, messy problem requires an unhinged, messy solution! A way to get creative with this is to conceptualize yourself as a beloved third person, then treating yourself thusly. In my own life, I have found great results by "tricking" my brain and my awareness into prioritizing my care by doing this "outsourcing" of self-love. After all, it can feel so much easier to care for others, so treating myself like a toddler or a lil' pet can do the trick when it comes to caring for myself.

You are a lovable little creature that could use some love and tending to. In your wildest state, stripped away from everything else and standing firmly in your authenticity, this is true. So find some feral self-care in giving yourself *exactly* what you need.

How to Do It

To begin "outsourcing" your self-love, it can help to get out a notebook and make a little primer on who and what you are and your needs for care. By making this fun with documented steps of your needs as though you are a third party, you may be more likely to check things off your self-love to do list! For example, you could write something like: "Mandi is a shy and creative creature who thrives on routine and enjoys cuddles, social time, and being fed on time" (obviously change this to suit yourself!).

Then make a list of your care needs or things you know will be loving acts of self-love and care, like:

- Creature needs to have daily walks.
- Creature needs to eat meals that are healthy and do not trigger food sensitivities.
- Creature needs to have social time at least twice per week.
- And so on.

The purpose of this is to find a creative way to lean into the idea that you are both the *caregiver* and the *cared for* and to have some fun with the true knowledge that you are a primal creature in need of love and care.

Gamify Your Self-Care

With a name like "self-care," you'd think it would be easy. After all, you *are* the self in question, right? Shouldn't you have a vested interest in how you're cared for? Although it may seem counterintuitive, for many, "self-care" isn't actually easy at all. In fact, you may be quite proficient at helping others while neglecting yourself altogether. What can explain this nonsensical bullshit, and how in the world did things get to be so backward?

Any given human life is fraught with multiple competing priorities, and for some reason self-care tasks or doing things that are fulfilling and supportive *just for you* typically find their way to the bottom of the list. Although this has been normalized in modern society, there are some obvious flaws in how this plays out. You cannot possibly have the mental and emotional space to do all the other things required of you if you are not being cared for yourself, yet for some reason you can still face this tricky resistance to putting yourself first.

Just like with any other responsibilities you may resist, you can find success in "gamifying" (adding game-like elements to) your self-care systems and routines in order to make them stick. After all, it's your silly, ridiculous brain and thought patterns that are in the way, so why not get some sneaky revenge by "tricking" them back into doing what really serves you?

Human motivation is tricky, but ultimately learning to hack your own motivational systems by using play and creativity can be fun and beneficial. When taking things seriously has you repeatedly hitting the wall and going nowhere, why not try something different, as off-beat and unconventional as it may sound?

Your unusual feral self-care tactic for getting out of your own damn way when it comes to self-care is this: Go forth and make it a fun game that you'll love to play with!

How to Do It

Gamify your self-care by incentivizing it in a fun way. Some examples are:

- **The rewards method:** Create a chart with a series of boxes or circles that correspond to the days in a month and then fill these in or "check" them each time you fulfill a self-care goal. Assign rewards for each series of days completed; for example, at the end of each week you could give yourself a small reward (like a fancy bubble bath) if you check off each day in that week, and then you could give yourself a bigger incentive, such as buying a new plant, for completing the month. You can make this as simple or as complex as you'd like; the important thing is to do it in the spirit of self-trust (no cheating!).
- **The visual representation method:** Take a jar and some things that are pleasant to look at. Fill up the jar with the nice-looking items as it corresponds with taking care of yourself. For example, add a dried flower blossom, a pretty rock, or something shiny to the jar when you do an act of self-care. At the end of your specified timeline, you will have an aesthetically pleasing visual representation of your progress.
- **The ceremonial method:** Choose a goal and track your progress. At the end, have yourself a "level completion" party or ceremony. Anything fun that is incentivizing for you and that essentially "thanks" and celebrates yourself for completion.

Set Boundaries Around Doomscrolling

As a modern human, how do you liberate yourself from the siren call of the doomscroll?

"Doomscrolling" is a term that refers to a behavior most are sadly familiar with: the excessive watching of the news/current events unfolding in real time. The "doom" comes from the fact that most of these events are negative or anxiety inducing, making them juicy targets of interest to suck you in under the guise that you want to "stay informed." It's *something a good modern citizen would do*!

However, doomscrolling is *not* the same as being informed. Here's the difference:

Staying informed is an intentional act *with* boundaries. You can check in to what's happening with the clear objective of gaining information. Many older folks remember when you could check the news at specific times of the day. That system had boundaries built in as you weren't able to watch the horrifying minutiae of whatever disaster was happening in an act of real-time play-by-play.

In contemporary times, you can access information 24/7. And while watching specific crises unfold in real time can *feel* like the responsible thing to do, it's just a way to avoid the free-floating anxiety that is in your body. It's doing *something* when you feel helpless and afraid. It's a digital "hand-wringing" of sorts.

The truth is that no amount of voyeuristic compassion is enhancing your own life experience, nor is it nobly solving any of the world's problems. All it's really doing is making things worse. *Your attention is your currency.* Entities literally profit from the behavior of doomscrolling. Every click and screen refresh triggers ad revenue and profit. So not only do you have the horror of constant knowledge in real time (something your mammalian brain and nervous system are not adapted to cope with), but this maladaptive behavior is also lining pockets.

As a creature of the wild, it is not selfish to give yourself boundaries when it comes to how often you interface with all the world's chaos. In fact, your mental health not only affects you but how you show up to the world. For your friends and family. For your kids if you have them.

So give yourself digital boundaries as an act of feral self-care. Your primal, animalistic nervous system could use it!

How to Do It

Give yourself permission to check in only at certain points in the day like people did back before the Internet got so loud. Create a structure of boundaries for yourself since the Internet and news at large won't do this for you. When it's your chosen time to dip into the world of the news and current events, perform a quick check-in with your mental and physical body to see if you have the space to do so. If not, put it off.

Are you privileged to be able to check in on the world? Unquestionably. *But* torching your mental health isn't going to give warmth to those in peril. Focus more on your own circle, your own life and loved ones, and the real-world actions you can take to help others and yourself. Give yourself permission to care *with* clear boundaries. Give yourself permission to take all that anxiety and fear and turn it into action that matters. Even if it's *just* in your own backyard.

Shake Up Your Environment

One thing about being human is that you are super influenced by the vibe of your surroundings. You can feel messy minded in cluttered spaces, calm out in nature, and uplifted in the presence of beauty. The state of your surroundings is actually key to your mood and mental states. This is valuable to know, especially when you're feeling bored and uninspired in your environments.

Humans can get bored easily, and the brain works in such a way that it can easily fall into autopilot and essentially "block out" the things that are familiar. Your home and spaces, when too familiar, can become "cues" for repetitive behaviors or habitual moods—that feeling of doing the same old shit at the same old time. Although there can be comfort in this sometimes, that hunk of electric chaos in your skull craves variety and the exciting vibe of shaking things up!

In my experience, I have better luck forming new habits when I start them somewhere fresh and new. For example, I enjoy healthy cooking more when I'm on vacation, I'm more likely to read or do daily stretching while I'm camping, and I find ease in tackling new routines right after I've cleaned or rearranged my home. The reason for this is simple: The brain gets lit up with new and novel things, and so it gets excited and enthusiastic about shaking things up to match the surrounding vibe!

Although cleaning and arranging your spaces differently can feel like a chore, the truth is that doing so can be an unusually potent source of self-care. A vibe check, if you will! Rearranging your spaces to shake up the flow of energy can be a fun and creative way to also shake you up internally. And sometimes for feral self-care this is exactly what you need!

How to Do It

Spend some time decluttering any spaces that feel like they are acting as an "energetic black hole." An "energetic black hole" doesn't even need to be a space you see visually every day. It could be that cabinet full of unfolded towels, the cupboard full of unsorted art supplies, or the space under the stairs that's full of...who even knows what! The reason that these act as "energetic black holes" is that although you may not always see them, you know that they are there, pulling on your awareness and adding to your mental load. When you clean these spaces up, you lighten the load and make room for more fulfilling concerns.

After decluttering, look at the "flow" of spaces where you feel stagnant energy-wise. These are rooms that you may spend a lot of time in but perhaps feel boring, uninspired, and like you gravitate toward automatic habits you'd like to let go of. Think of some ways you can shake up these spaces so they tickle your subconscious awareness in novel and exciting ways! This can be done with new art or decor, changing the arrangement of the furniture, or simply shifting around what "stuff" is in there.

Adorn Yourself

When I was younger, I would gaze longingly at those who were wildly and outwardly creative. Those who were pierced, tattooed, wearing loud and unique clothing, those whose style was so wholly unconventional it would trigger those who *just didn't get it*. I was attracted to the style, the vibes, but more importantly to the concept that there are those out there that comfortably and enthusiastically did as they pleased with nary a fuck to be given to what some bare-minimum bitch was going to think!

The only thing that they had that I did not (yet) was the courage and the self-assuredness to just...do it! There is truly nothing different between the person who hides and the person who is loudly and audaciously themselves except a willingness to *choose* their own wild self-expression, giving it priority over the very human drive to stay small and fit in. To put it plainly, the authentic expression of those living loudly, and the happiness and freedom it invokes, must be more compelling than being perceived as "acceptable."

Now, maybe you aren't into the strange and unusual outward expression of individuality—not everyone is. But chances are you *are* into something that you are holding as off-limits for yourself in some way. There may be *some avenue* in which you are holding back when it comes to your style or authentic expression in order to feel safe. After all, breaking the mold and expressing yourself can be immensely vulnerable. It's basically laying yourself out on the table, unguarded and exposed and saying, "This is who I am," flirting with the possibility of rejection and judgment that may follow.

The ability to move in alignment with your wildest, most unhinged expression is proportionate to how much you confidently love and value yourself. Which is great news because confidence and loving self-acceptance are always within your reach! This remains true even if just reading that sentence made you feel a whole-body "*hell* no" (I see you!). It simply takes some work and mental exploration. For example, reminding yourself that there is only *this one life* where you can either thrive for yourself or dim for judgments that aren't even guaranteed.

So if you want to feel comfortable in expressive style, both loudly and vulnerably visible, then find some feral self-care in adorning yourself the way you see fit. You are both the work of art and the artist—this is true for all elements of your true, authentic self, including your aesthetics!

How to Do It

Create a vision board of the aesthetic you're drawn to and begin to play around with ways you can show up in that style when you are at home, safely in private. See how it feels, and gradually examine any barriers you have to confidently show up as...well...*you*! Work your way up to adorning yourself the way you want in more public settings.

As you work to express yourself, know this: One day the people you are trying to tiptoe about and not capture the attention of will be dead and gone. And unfortunately...so will you. You will not get any award for living your life small; instead, you may be left with the regret of not having let your authenticity shine.

So go balls to the wall and adorn yourself in whatever way feels best! Do it for yourself as an act of liberating feral self-care.

CHAPTER 6

The Village Around You:

EMBRACING THE HUMAN NEED FOR COMMUNITY

Thanks to social media and advanced tech, the modern human experience is simultaneously connected *and* lonely. You may have heard the phrase "losing the village," as the contemporary way of life seems to be hyperindividual, with little space for community structures. But community care and relying on the support of social networks is a dimension of the human experience that goes back through the ages. When human beings lived in smaller communal circles, they shared the load more when it came to resource collection, caregiving, and general everyday responsibilities. To be social is a fundamental human need, and people have evolved over time to crave community, to rely on it, and to be fulfilled in the experiences of sharing their lives in loving relationships.

Although human relationships can be messy and unpredictable, both the positive and negative aspects of community are necessary for growth, happiness, and self-care. There is great healing potential in social relationships and shared experiences. So let's turn toward embracing the proverbial village once more as an act of feral self-care. In this chapter, you will celebrate your tendency toward community and liberate yourself from the restrictions of trying to do it all alone.

Ask for Help

Even though humans are prosocial creatures that thrive in community, when it comes to asking for help, it's easy to hold back. If you were to sit and reflect at this moment about how comfortable you are *giving* help to others versus asking for help yourself, what would you feel? In many cases people are better at giving than receiving and certainly flounder the most when it comes to reaching out and asking.

Although you may know deep down in your heart that there is no shame in asking for help—after all, you certainly can find a lot of joy in giving it—something deep down tends to include a caveat of "not for me though." And this is certainly backed up in modern culture. The fabled "village" that you hear of needing in order to survive is largely gone, replaced by a sense of individualism and the pervasive myth of the person who can "do it all."

While it is true that you are a dazzling, unique individual who is strong and capable of many amazing things, the entire concept of doing it all alone is a fucking lie. And a damaging one at that! You are meant to have a community, and you are meant to lean on that community when necessary. It's okay to ask for help, and doing so isn't coming from a place of lack or weakness. It's actually a formidable act of strength and a recognition of what it means to be human.

Asking for help can be one of the most loving acts of self-care you can give yourself. It honors your raw humanity, as it honors the very special role that your friendships and communities have in your experience of this one wild and chaotic life.

How to Do It

Practice asking for help in safe spaces with safe people. These are your "ride or die" people—friends and family, those that you know would be there for you in an instant, even if it came at an inconvenience to themselves. The purpose of this is to get your nervous system stable when it comes to asking. Practice makes perfect!

The kind of help you can ask for can range from small asks that don't require a lot of effort on the helper's end (but mean a lot to you) to larger asks that are more labor- or energy-intensive. For example, a small ask may be a request for your friends to check in on you during a difficult time period, and a larger ask may include things like asking for help moving from one apartment to another. The most important thing is for *you* as the asker to have a solid grasp of the type of help you need and what will be most meaningful to you.

Although it may sound crazy in the context of current society, asking for help with things like cleaning the house, meal planning, or other mundane tasks is actually super normal. This is shit everyone struggles with, so why not come together? And if you struggle to ask, then think of this: If someone asked you for help, would you be upset about it? Or maybe would you be just so happy to help someone you love and care about so much that you would be honored to be asked?

Now extend that same grace to yourself.

Get in Touch with Where Your Food Comes From

One of the biggest chasms between current society and the way things used to be is the distance between people and food. As things have become increasingly global, you now as a consumer don't always know where your food comes from. Most people roam the brightly lit grocery stores for food, a far cry from the past of foraging and hunting it. And although my own lazy ass is thankful for the convenience, there is something to be said about the kind of self-care that comes from having a deeper relationship to your food.

Luckily, even in many of the most industrialized modern areas, there is access to local food that can help you bridge this gap. Many cities and communities have things like farmers' markets, local farms, butchers, artisans' markets, and more. Often, these are also more sustainable options, as these sorts of businesses typically have a reduced environmental impact. Although there can be some cost and convenience variation in shopping like this, you can also feel more connected to your food and local communities—two things that can increase your quality of life significantly.

Now, it's important to note that there is nothing wrong with shopping at the grocery store or buying packaged or processed food. Everyone is doing their best just trying to survive out here! However, there is a special kind of human connectedness that comes with forging a relationship to where food comes from, which can include getting to know the people and families that feed you and your communities. It's something that is hard to describe in words but easy to identify when you feel it. It feels like community, simplicity, and like tapping into a forgotten dimension of humanity.

So get in touch with your local food community as a radical act of feral self-care! Just because you exist in this modern world of convenience doesn't mean that you can't explore in the realm of local food communities and get back to basics when it comes to forging connections and relationships through food!

How to Do It

Get involved in your local food community! Support local crafters, artisans, and farmers whenever possible. This support could be in the form of buying from them or simply sharing about their wares. While it's true that supporting local can be pricier due to the increased costs associated with doing small business (small businesses and organizations don't get anywhere near the help and breaks that the behemoth "too big to fail" monstrosities do), there are some workarounds, such as budgeting to make space for this and also keeping in mind that it isn't an all-or-nothing endeavor. It *is* possible to both support your local communities and still shop at larger convenience stores. There is something very important about knowing where your food comes from and supporting the local farms and vendors in your area. It can be not only a healthier and more sustainable endeavor, but it can also help the health of the community at large.

Local food communities and the connections they foster are a treasure, and you should support them whenever you can. Not only for your own individual feral self-care but for society as a whole!

Gather Over Food

If there's one thing about humans, it's that they love to get together, throw big parties, and *eat*! To get together over food and drink and laugh and sort out dramas has been a part of tradition across cultures for ages. It's typically regarded as one of the hallmarks of civilization itself. And from birthday parties to spiritual ceremonies, feasting together is one ritualistic and primal human behavior that has continued into the modern era.

Anthropologists have studied feasting ceremonies and traditions to find out the specific role they've played in the development and evolution of human culture. To engage in feasting requires organization and a sharing of resources. And the presence of these ceremonies or gatherings creates the perfect place to plan, be entertained, engage in ritual, and just generally do cooperative social human things. For this reason, feasting, or the act of eating and drinking together, has stood the test of time.

Much like gathering around a fire is a primal human behavior, so too is the tendency to gather over food as a gesture of community and sociality. The fact that this is a behavior that continues across cultures and across time is evidence that this is an endeavor of primal importance. It is a wildly human undertaking! Humans are a social species that thrives in community. And sometimes, giving yourself this opportunity to gather in community is a gift of self-care to yourself.

So your feral self-care assignment is to dip into the undomesticated human urge to feast together in groups! Plan a gathering over food and drink as an act of feral self-care and fellowship.

How to Do It

Host a social gathering that centers around the sharing of food and drink as an act of feral self-care. In sharing food, you will get to have the unique fulfillment and joy that comes with sharing the experience—particularly if those who come also bring something meaningful to them to share! Even when it's a potluck-style dinner party where everyone brings their own dish of some sort, it can be helpful to organize things even loosely so that you don't end up with a single salad and seven desserts. It is even possible to do one theme; some examples would be:

- Bring a dish from your childhood.
- Bring a dish from your culture.
- Bring a dish that corresponds with a special memory.
- Bring a dish that's a conversation starter.

The main thing is to do this activity in the spirit of gratitude—gratitude for the food available, the spirit of sharing, and the gift of good people to share it with!

Be Honest

Nobody likes a liar; however, everyone lies. This is just part and parcel of living in a polite social society. Although honesty is something to be valued, and a good quality to strive for, in practice a totally honest world perhaps wouldn't be as comfortable and prosocial as some would like to believe. Honesty is messy and leaves a lot of space left wide open for hurt feelings and conflict—things that are also valuable but sometimes best left avoided. So the key to honesty is much like anything else in this life: It's an exercise in balance and clear intentions.

You likely engage in small, socially sanctioned lies all day, every day. This helps you be more sociable, find belonging in groups, and just generally get along with others. For example, you may find yourself telling small lies to avoid hurting someone's feelings or crushing their enthusiasm. You may also lie to *yourself* more often than you are likely aware of. This is more of a psychological coping mechanism, and one that has the potential to do you some good in many ways. For example, if you want good things to happen, you have to be a little bit "positively delusional," which means assuming that things are going to work out so you don't fall into a pit of despair.

However, not all the "little lies" you tell others or yourself are doing you any favors. Conflict and hurt feelings can be like carbon under pressure: a potential source for valuable "diamonds" in the shape of lessons learned, deepened relationships, and more. As with most things in this drama-fueled experience of life, the more you embrace the hard parts head-on, the less likely you are to face even more conflict and bullshit later!

To be radically honest is a very primal and feral thing: It requires you to strip away the civilized ideas that you must stay small and act nice to get along. It asks you to be brave and to elevate your relationships to a level of intimacy that may be uncomfortable but ultimately worthwhile and rewarding.

So if you're looking for some interpersonal feral self-care, find safe spaces to be radically honest.

How to Do It

The next time you are having an issue with a friend or loved one where you feel the familiar desire to stuff your feelings back into the trunk, resist doing so. Particularly if doing so would be to your own detriment. Ultimately, honesty in uncomfortable situations can sometimes be a great way to lay your cards on the table and get on the same page with someone. It can also be a great way to see where you stand with that person. If you are afraid to share your feelings with someone because of how they will respond, that might be a big, glaring red flag.

If radical honesty is totally new for you, it can help to make a statement such as "I am playing around with being more honest about how things impact me or make me feel." Doing this can also prime your conversation partner so they are prepared for you to spit some honesty. This can be helpful as well in cases where you also need to be honest with *yourself*. For example, times where you can share something like "I am feeling X type of way, even though I know it is irrational and a personal issue." This is being honest with yourself while also giving insight to a loved one about what you are going through that they may not be aware of.

Weave the Village

Sometimes, self-care is less about the "self" and more about finding belonging and inclusion as part of a whole. As human society has shifted and evolved through the ages, it seems to have moved further away from the concept of the "village" (smaller groups and communities that both live with and help each other).

Wellness has been impacted greatly by this distancing from the smaller intimate communities of the past. Although we may be highly connected in the digital sense, we can still feel isolated, and the mental health of humans overall seems to have declined alongside the "progress" into a society where, on an individual level, many feel disconnected and unsupported. Humans are creatures of the wild, and it is part of your primal nature to have communities with others where you can help and be helped, solve problems, and unite for the common good.

It is this concept of the "village" that has helped the species get to where it is at. And even though modern society has stretched so communities are less intimate and social circles are far wider, that doesn't mean that your desire and natural tendency to crave smaller communities has disappeared. Your human nature longs for these spaces, and it's what drives you to gravitate toward like-minded people and form friendships and more intimate social circles.

Luckily, just because you live in this modern society, that doesn't mean that you don't have the ability to weave these smaller groups for yourself. At any given point you can start building your own little subcommunities to help others and be helped. In fact, these naturally seem to occur in places where humans exist together, such as in neighborhoods, workspaces, or in groups that collect over common interests (farmers' markets are a good example of small communities).

As a method of feral self-care, form your own circles or small communities. Whether this be over a common purpose or interest or to achieve some aim, you will find yourself indulging in activities and relationships that can feel immensely fulfilling and purposeful while also providing support and companionship that you crave.

How to Do It

To start a smaller community, try to think of some aspect of life that could benefit from forming a "village" around for camaraderie and support. These villages can be for anything really, but a common theme is that they are often purposeful in some way. Some examples:

- Local sustainable food communities: Supporting or trading with like-minded people for food, prepared goods, and other things that support the spirit of shopping local rather than inflating large corporate profits.
- Spiritual/personal development communities: Healing circles, moon gatherings, spiritual workshops, retreats, etc.
- Child-rearing communities: Sharing knowledge and resources for caring or schooling your children, leaning on other parents for resources, emotional support or help, organizing "field trips" for experiential learning, organizing get-togethers for moms who are suffering from loneliness, meal trains, etc.

Brainstorm your own ideas and set about bringing them to life!

Indulge In a Nourishing Embrace

One thing about human beings is they *need* touch. Touch is not only just a sense that allows you to experience the world, but human touch (touch that occurs *between* people) is necessary for your well-being. From the moment you are born, it is vital to your very health and survival that you experience the primal benefit of touch, and this continues across your lifespan. There has been much research done on the benefits of human touch showing that it can calm us down and make our brains release pleasurable, feel-good chemicals. The results are pretty damn clear: The human creature needs to both touch and *be* touched!

However, even though this is a vital need, it is not always available. Socially, this concept can be tricky. For human beings, touch is incredibly personal. It's an intimate act that typically requires some level of trust and closeness to occur. You certainly aren't free to just go around touching other people all willy-nilly! There has to be consent, comfort for all parties, and also a shared concept of what is appropriate or socially acceptable in the realm of human touch.

For example, handshaking is a kind of touch that is generally considered a low-intimacy gesture. However, hugging might be considered a high-intimacy gesture, depending on the person you ask. Touching may be considered normal or expected in a romantic setting, but your mileage may vary when it comes to platonic touch between friends. Touching a stranger might be a lawsuit waiting to happen, unless you are a massage therapist, in which case things change! There are so many variables that play in when it comes to meeting this need, but the need itself is legit: You just gotta have that human touch!

When it comes to self-care, it's easy to get hung up on what you can do for yourself. But some of the best self-care involves shifting your attitude toward how you relate to others. In this case, it might be worth examining: How do you view touch? Is it awkward? Acceptable? A sensory "fuck no"? Only to happen between lovers? How does this view impact the amount of touch that you have available to you? Has it been helpful to you or not?

For some feral self-care, look at the presence of nourishing embrace in your life. Everyone carries the deep need to be touched physically, so what could that look like for you?

How to Do It

Reflect on the presence of touch in your life.

It's possible that you may have a physically affectionate partner, friend group, or family, in which case this may not be an issue. If these are your circumstances, feel free to dole out hugs and snuggles like it's going out of style. Genuinely appreciate and sink into the connection that they give you. Let yourself feel grateful that this gets to be a part of your human experience!

If you are in a situation where you feel touch starved (also known as "skin hunger" or "touch deprivation," which is exactly what it sounds like), examine where this lack stems from. It could be an aversion to touch, which is totally valid, or it could be a lack of safe or trusted people in your life to engage in this practice with. In the latter case, you could seek out alternatives, such as cuddling a pet, getting a massage, or engaging in a self-massage practice similar to the Do a Self-Massage activity discussed in Chapter 3.

Find Self-Care in Caregiving

Human beings are prosocial, which means the species has thrived by helping each other. Despite the fact that you can leave the comments section of social media feeling like the majority of humans are trash, the truth is typically the opposite: When face-to-face with each other, people carry deep instincts to be helpful in order to gain the trust and acceptance of the group. In many cases, you may feel even *more* comfortable taking steps to help others than you do to help yourself. For those who have a "caregiver" archetype personality, helping others can give the kind of benefits and good feelings that you'd think caring for yourself should, such as improved mood and enhanced life satisfaction.

In a roundabout way, sometimes self-care can come from caring for *others*! Now you might be thinking, "How can taking care of others be considered an act of true self-care?" Well, the answer brings up the old philosophical question: *Is there such a thing as a truly selfless act?* Every time you extend yourself to help others, you unquestionably benefit in some way. Whether it be the external validation you get or the internal fulfillment that comes from a genuinely kind act.

Some can find themselves putting others first consistently. Although it can feel like a drag sometimes, there *must* be a reason they persist. On some level, they are getting some benefit from putting other people first even when it's at a detriment to themselves. All behavior fills a need, and so if a behavior is persisting, there is *something* they are surely getting from it, some need it is fulfilling, even if that reason is buried in the sub-basement of conscious awareness. In many cases, this behavior is helping the person who is giving the care feel good about themselves, whether it be through the validation and recognition they get from others or simply the internal satisfaction that comes from doing something nice for others.

Now, the key to getting empowered self-care through caring for others is to find a healthy outlet for it. No martyr vibes allowed, baby! If caring for others is something that satisfies and fulfills your creature needs for love and community, it is imperative that you find a way to help and care for others that won't be draining, where you won't be taken advantage of, and that is actually welcome (nobody likes an overbearing helping hand).

So find some fun in helping your fellow human. You may be surprised what a radical (although somewhat odd) form of self-care this is!

How to Do It

Allow yourself a healthy release for the desires you have to care for others. Some ideas to get you started are:

- Caring for your friends who might be having a hard time.
- Volunteering your time to help those in need.
- Making things of value and use that you can give away to those who need them.
- Creating things for the people you love.
- Offering your time and support with regular life stuff (cooking, cleaning, etc.) for the people in your life who could use some extra help.

There are a variety of ways that you can find to use your caregiving urges to help those in need, which, in turn, will help you feel good too!

Accept Help

Earlier in this chapter, you explored the importance of asking for help. In modern "every man for himself" culture, it can be truly a struggle to break free of the individualistic vibe that encourages doing it all alone. Yet, as you have learned, asking for help can be a powerful form of self-care. Of course, asking for help is one thing; being able to actually *accept* help that is offered and given is wildly another. This is another skill that can be as equally confounding as asking for help.

For many, accepting help from others feels foreign and can trigger old wounds that come from childhood experiences and social conditioning. Deep down inside your messy soul, you may struggle to believe that offers of help are things to be accepted and not just another chance for you to prove you're committed to being "tough" or to "not being a bother."

But, dear creature, please believe that you can be safe in taking up space and accepting the help that is being offered, enthusiastically and without shame!

You get no trophies or awards for doing it all on your own. You do not make yourself more worthy or lovable by burning yourself to the ground in order to "do it all" alone. Truly, everyone loses when you hold yourself off from allowing communities to love and support you. You cut others off from the benefit of getting to shower you with their kindness, and you cut yourself off from having an easier go of it by letting them. And please believe that when help is offered, it's because people truly *want* to love and support you.

Your next feral self-care strategy is to accept the help that those around you are willing to give. Allow others to love and support you, and don't stand in your own (and their!) damn way.

How to Do It

Allow yourself to find peace and care in accepting the help that is offered to you!

One thing that can help is this: Reflect on the last time you offered help to someone. Were you just talking out of your ass, or did you actually *mean* it? It's actually incredibly easy to hear about what someone is going through and say nothing or simply nod your head and listen in an act of support and solidarity. Should someone offer something more than that, whether it be some sort of concrete action or emotional support, it is because they truly want to help. And although it can be hard for you to accept (or even comprehend) that people want to help you, explore for a moment the idea that this person extending love and kindness for you is telling the truth. That they *do* want to help you. That they value and care for you so much that doing so would be their pleasure.

You are a loved and valuable creature that is so supported. So give yourself some feral self-care in allowing yourself to shamelessly and enthusiastically accept the help that is offered to you!

Enjoy Platonic Intimacy

Intimacy is so important. Humans have a deep desire to burrow into relationships, to find warmth and safety in the loving context of community, in the opportunity to be truly "seen" and understood by others.

Although many think of intimacy in the context of romance, there is so much more to it than that. The word "intimacy" is defined as a feeling of connection, closeness, and security with another person. You can have this kind of unconditionally fulfilling support from many other places beyond the boundaries of romantic love. If you are lucky, you may experience this with your family members or your closest friends. And if you *have* felt this kind of intimacy in your relationships, then its presence in your life should be celebrated and cherished!

Platonic intimacy is found in those kinds of nonromantic connections. It can be seen in your most supportive and close friendships and, in some cases, in the relationships you have with your family. Platonic intimacy is special because it asks for nothing of you. There are no tricky sexual waters to navigate and no expectations. It is a pure kind of love, one that your life can be greatly enhanced by having known.

A key aspect of inviting in platonic intimacy is vulnerability—that juicy dimension of interpersonal relationships that make them so frightful and compelling. For true intimacy, you are required to let your guard down. And although this can be immensely difficult, in doing so you can make way for some of the most fulfilling and beautiful relationships possible.

Although you may tend to retreat or play it cool in your friendships, there is much to be achieved by having deep, fulfilling, and vulnerable connections. So as a form of feral self-care, lean into the special, rare beauty of platonic intimacy. You are meant to form full and meaningful relationships, and you honor a wild and beautiful kind of connection in doing so.

How to Do It

There are a variety of ways that you can lean into your primal nature and form platonic intimacy with others. Some examples are:

- Forming a wellness "coven" (a circle of friends exploring personal growth and spiritual development).
- Hugging your friends! Snuggle them if they're cool with it. Never ever be afraid to make it weird.
- Having weekly cry and/or scream circles.
- Writing platonic love letters—express your appreciation for the deepest parts of who they are.
- Truly listening to your friends.
- Sharing your deepest thoughts and hopes and dreams with those who are safe for you.
- Most importantly, giving love freely and authentically. Allow yourself to be loved the same in return. Let yourself revel in both loving and being loved!

Try out these different ways of forming platonic intimacy, or brainstorm your own ideas and start building those pure connections.

Let People Go

Everyone has felt it: When you find someone who lights you up and truly sees you, it can be the most exciting thing in the world. Forming relationships with others can be a real thrill, but in many cases people are not in your life to stay. As a conscious human being, you are constantly growing and evolving, and sometimes this means growing apart from the people you've loved and cherished. As sad as this can be, it's just a fact of life and can happen with lovers, friends, and even family members.

When people grow apart, it can be devastating. Especially because this doesn't always correspond with some big event or grand betrayal. In some cases, the reason for a relationship to dissolve is fairly clear, while in others there is a slow fizzling out that can leave you feeling confused and lost. Any time you experience a relationship that was once close become fractured, it is hurtful regardless of circumstances. Which means many people tend to keep relationships they've outgrown or where they are not being treated right in the interest of holding on to something that feels scary to let go of.

Some people are not meant to be in your awareness in perpetuity. Some people's place in your life has a clear end date, and you need to learn when to let the dead connections die. Although it can hurt to let some of your relationships go, sometimes doing this is an act of self-care, particularly in the cases where the person is no longer good for you. This isn't to say that you should go pushing people out of your life all willy-nilly, but there is something to be said about recognizing when a relationship is toxic or has run its course and taking steps to release that relationship with love and gratitude.

Sometimes you can find big feral self-care benefits in accepting the way things are even if this is different from what you wanted. Authenticity isn't only a quality you possess but also something found in accepting the reality of whatever situation you are in. So let people go when it's time to do so as an act of self-care. Whether you are letting them go with love or with grief, the important thing is to do this with a shit ton of compassion for yourself.

How to Do It

To begin, reflect on your relationships and whether there are any that you are holding on to even though they have run their course. Chances are, if there is one that fits the bill, it would have popped into your head while reading this very entry.

Any time you embark on a journey of letting someone go, whether it be through a breakup or going no contact with a family member, it's important to do so in the spirit of gentle kindness. Kindness for yourself and kindness for the other person. In many cases, there will be no need for judgment or anger: You can release people in the spirit of compassion and evolution. Sometimes this is the best act of respect you can do for the relationship that was—to put it out of its misery!

It's also important to remember that this doesn't necessarily mean that you are letting that person go forever. Many people have had experiences where others will cycle in and out of their life orbits throughout time, growing and evolving both together and separately. However, how far you leave the door open—or whether it remains open at all—is up to you.

Engage in Co-Creation

As discussed a lot throughout this book, the human consciousness is an incredibly powerful, creative machine. You have the knack to pull things from the imagination space and manifest them into reality in a way that's like magic. And as many creative people know, sometimes you can create unexpectedly magical things when you engage in community. The power of co-creation, or creating by using the ideas, creative flow, and consciousness of more than one human, can be powerful, fulfilling, and healing all at the same time.

Although you may think of creating as this thing you sit down with and do with purpose, the truth is that you are *always* creating. Whenever I hear people say they don't consider themselves creative, I ask them to reflect on what was the last batshit crazy, anxiety-driven scenario they dreamt up. That is an act of creation! The truth is you are creating constantly, even if you have no tangible art skills to show for it. Every time you daydream, you are creating. Every time you fix your sights on a goal, you are creating. Even when you decide what you want less of in life, this is creating. And creating in this manner is not always done alone. Every time you do these things by processing with others, you are engaging in co-creation that has the potential to help you shift your circumstances and refine your intentions with the loving support of others.

The act of engaging in imaginative co-creation can be a truly deep and significant way for humans to not only bring creations to life but to tap into an underrated form of intimacy that can be beautifully fulfilling. Part of the feral self-care method is to weave chaos—what better way to weave your chaos than to ask a friend to help out? So your next feral self-care task is to shamelessly engage in co-creation with a trusted person you love. To do so is primally human and can have big returns in both your relationships and your life.

How to Do It

Engaging in co-creation is something that you may already be doing intuitively in your relationships. For example, when you and your partner dream up your future life, you are engaging in co-creating the future you want to see. Similarly, when you go to a friend to hash out your goals or creative ideas, and you bounce off each other, turning that glimmer of something into a concept that is more clearly refined, it is co-creation. However, co-creation can be tangible too. Maybe you and a friend can co-create a workshop or routine together. Maybe you can work together on an art project or social offering. Choose something to co-create right now with someone in your life!

It's important to note that co-creation can be vulnerable and intimate in terms of ego. This is an act that should be done with people you love and trust and who support you. Sometimes it can muddy the vision to co-create with those who may limit or sabotage your excitement about a particular dream or project. This doesn't necessarily mean those people are bad, just that they may not be the best partner for you to co-create with.

Share an Experience You Love

One of the most beautiful aspects of this wild and messy life is the connections that you make. Although there is beauty in independence and self-reliance, making true connections with others can be one of the most fulfilling experiences. It's a dance of giving and receiving when you become comfortable with someone. Even the most platonic relationships are a delicious smorgasbord of sharing the important pieces of you, and it's in this sharing of yourself that you can find some of the most valuable connections. This includes the very intimate act of sharing the experiences you love.

As a human being, the person you feel that you are is one of the most sacred things. Your identity helps form your self-concept, and every time you open up to others it requires letting your guard down. Although it's easy to take it for granted, any time you share who you are with others, show them the things you love, or let them into your unique little world, you are doing something immensely brave and vulnerable. As a social critter, you put yourself at risk: Will they like me? Will they accept me? Will sharing who I authentically am scare them away?

Sharing an experience you love with someone else is deeply meaningful. It isn't just "doing something together"; it is a whole special way to show and express love for yourself *and* for a trusted other. It's taking something that's meaningful to you, laying it on the table, and saying, "I want you to share this with me." Whether this be as simple as a movie or song you like or something more involved, like your favorite hobby, *all* of it is a gesture of love.

To go feral is to break down barriers that hold you off from your authenticity. So, you can find some vital self-care in sharing who you are with those you love, even if that means exposing the soft underbelly of who you are. Sharing experiences with others can be a sacred space where you display your heart and dive into the messy vulnerability of being seen by someone else.

How to Do It

Sharing an experience with someone you love and trust is just as simple as it sounds! If there is an activity or experience that has been meaningful and important for you, invite someone who is also meaningful and important to you to come join in. Simple thing(s) you share could include:

- A book that had an important impact on you.
- A song or playlist that is meaningful for you.
- A TV show that is special to you.
- Photos from an impactful event in your life.

What you share can also be more involved. Some other ways you can share an experience with another are:

- Taking a friend to a place that has special significance for you, such as on a hike or to a meaningful location.
- Allowing a friend to come and do a beloved hobby with you, such as painting or ceramics.
- Going on a retreat or vacation with someone.
- Doing a class or learning something important together.
- Sharing your art.

Whatever it is, do it together in the spirit of love and authenticity! After all, who you are in all your authentic glory is the greatest thing you can share with those you love!

Commit to Sharing Your Authentic Self

Although it sounds counterintuitive, showing up exactly as who you authentically are can be a fucking struggle. Logically, being who you truly are seems like it would be the path of least resistance, but unfortunately this makes a lot more sense in theory than in practice. As a social creature, you can often find your true expression limited by thoughts of how those around you will receive you. And as an emotional creature (with a tendency to think way too much), you can often flail around wondering who you really are in the first place!

Sadly, your own needs and desire to live life on your own terms are too often pushed to the side in society. The tendency to put a lid on the fullest, biggest, most audacious version of yourself has been somewhat normalized. The programming is subtle, but it's all around: You can see it in movies, TV shows, and the average response to pop culture in media, forums, etc. The human species is naturally judgmental, and the evidence of that can leave you feeling a little bit wary of "rocking the boat." Everywhere you look, it seems like you are given the same message: It's really just best for everyone if you shut up, stay small, and fit in.

Well, the thrilling and terrifying truth is that this, like most societally enforced ideals, is pure, unadulterated bullshit! Being true to who you are in an authentically real way may ruffle some feathers, sure, but ultimately it is well worth the struggle. After all, shouldn't your own happiness and desires regarding how to live take precedence over the comfort of some random dude who wishes you were more "normal"? Other people do not get to tell you who you are; you *choose*!

So commit yourself to sharing the authentic fullness of your truth as an act of radical liberation and feral self-care! Because at the end of the day, any energy you spend fighting your true nature is time that's essentially wasted. The world is full of stuff that is going to drain your energy and happiness if you let it; you simply do not have extra gas in the tank to spend hiding yourself!

How to Do It

Set an intention that you are going to focus your commitment to showing up in a way that feels good and right for you, rooted in your authenticity.

Create a "commitment ritual" to yourself as a way to solidify your intent to share your authentic self with the world. This sends a subliminal message to yourself that *you* are choosing *you*. In our society, commitment ceremonies are fairly customary (marriages, swearing oaths, etc.); however, it's highly unusual to do them for ourselves. Well, perhaps committing to ourselves in a formalized way is exactly what we need to solidify our intentions to put our best interests first!

Some examples:

- Create a contract with yourself promising to share your authenticity.
- Create a ritual of "burning away" any resistance you feel on the path to sharing your authenticity.
- Use a mirror to verbally state aloud your commitment to sharing your free and authentic self.
- Set up a creative "commitment ceremony" to yourself, much like a wedding, but in this case as a marriage between you and your truth. Make the sharing of your authenticity the "other half" of yourself, so that in showing up in your authenticity, you are showing up as whole.

No matter what you choose to do, just know that the important thing is to value yourself enough to commit to the messy task of prioritizing this commitment. Of all the promises you have made to people, the ones you make to yourself have just as much value and merit, if not more!

CHAPTER 7

A Return to Spirit:
ACKNOWLEDGING THE SPIRITUAL DIMENSION OF HUMAN NATURE

While your animal nature is primal and physical, logical and emotional, there is another dimension of humanity that emerges from your feral wildness. This is the dimension of spirit. Spirituality isn't just about structured religion; it is about connectedness, mystery, and the very human tendency to find meaning in the unknown. Just because mainstream society often holds spirituality at arm's length doesn't mean you as a human do not carry a deep need for it. In fact, when not given an outlet or permission to be expressed, people can end up finding meaning and purpose in meaningless and purposeless things as a substitute. This is how many get sucked into "choosing sides" and identifying too strongly with things that may not truly matter for wellness.

To return to spirit is to find something deeply fulfilling deep in your primal core. Through doing so you honor your true nature, find peace and self-care, and embrace your mystical wild. In this final chapter you will dive into this spiritual dimension of life, finding primal meaning and calm connectedness in the hectic drama of modern-day life.

Burn an Effigy

Something unique about the human animal is that your consciousness allows you to tap into the realm of the symbolic. By using symbolic association and understanding, you can create sacred rituals for yourself, categorize things for enhanced understanding, and find ways to examine issues you face beyond the dimension of the obvious.

A great example of this very human tendency to play with the power of symbol is the idea of "burning an effigy." This is a theme that has been played out in many cultural traditions and rituals and can be seen often in entertainment and media. An effigy is traditionally a statue or model to represent a specific person. In the case of ritualistically burning an effigy, the model created stands as the representation of the real person. For feral self-care purposes however, it is less about the symbolic act of burning someone in particular and more about the symbol of release that this practice represents. In this case, the effigy is not another person but a representation of some aspect of life, circumstances, or the self that you can sacrifice to the fire for the greater good!

As a witch, I personally use the practice of burning effigies as a symbolic way to release bad habits, things I want gone from my life, or as a way to symbolize that I'm ready to "kill" the person that I was to become the person that I'm ready to be. To burn something in effigy, specifically something that is under your control and that has the power to enhance your life experience, is a truly empowered act. It is also an act that is energetically backed by its deep history of use, and in burning something in effigy, you can awaken something primal and powerful within you.

So the next time you are feeling like you need to release something in a powerful and meaningful way, put it to fire in an act of feral self-care.

How to Do It

Plan a fire to symbolically burn up something you're trying to release, for example:

- A bad habit you want to let go of.
- An attachment or person you want to release.
- Something you have been "stuck" on or ruminating over.
- A mindset barrier you want to push past.
- A piece of you/your personality that you are ready to leave behind.

Obviously, ensure that you are practicing safety, such as using a fire pit with a lid and using materials that won't release any toxic fumes, etc.

Although there are a variety of ways you can approach this practice creatively, the simplest method is to write down or draw what you are trying to release. After doing this, affirm to yourself or state your intention to release the thing. Then, to burn what you want to release in effigy, take your paper (or whatever you've made your effigy from) and toss into the fire.

Burn the things that no longer serve you in a rebelliously and spiritually potent act of wild, empowered mysticism.

Make a Date with Your Intuition

As a human being, you have many super abilities and skills. One of these is your power of intuition. Although intuition is a sense that is typically scoffed at in the modern rationalist paradigm, the truth is that you are powerfully gifted and aided by this invisible sense. Intuition can be defined as an "inner knowing" that you possess even when you do not have clear evidence for *how* or *why* you know it. It is a feeling, a sense, something wholly natural and yet simultaneously unexplainable.

Primally speaking, the power to tap into this ability is a gift of your very humanity itself. Just as you have the power to reason and think, so too do you have the power to be intuitively guided should you be open to it. All it really takes is a little cultivation and openness as well as some time and some training to learn what it is, how it feels, and how to essentially "speak its language."

Part of the process of deconditioning yourself from the modern paradigm is learning when to shut the fuck up and connect with the guidance you have available within. Your awareness is so consistently hijacked with the consumption of content that the noise can be unbearable. You need to slow way down and connect with the quiet little voice within that is dying to be heard and helpful!

To allow yourself the time and space to be guided by your intuition is a powerful act of feral self-care. It takes a certain amount of self-trust to take that voice seriously, and as you learn to listen carefully you might find yourself surprised by just how often it may help you! So take some time regularly to silence the noise and connect to the mystical whisper of your intuitive senses.

How to Do It

1. Begin each "intuition date" by turning off your phone or any other devices that may distract or hijack your awareness.
2. Find a space where you feel comfortable and secure and are unlikely to be disturbed. Then just...sit. Alone. With yourself.
3. Place no expectations on what you think should and could happen during this practice, and instead focus simply on what does happen. What feelings do you get? What messages do you hear? What exactly do you feel in your body?

Depending on how underutilized your intuition is, you may end up feeling silly or like nothing has happened at all when first trying this. However, every moment spent doing this is time well spent, and you will start hearing and feeling more with each date.

In the modern world particularly, you rarely actually get the time, space, and silence required to connect with your intuition and feel truly present in your body. Which means you are often cut off from one of the most reliable and customized sources of guidance available to you! So make little dates in silence with the faithful companion that is your intuition. It is here that you will open the doors to one of the most powerful gifts that your humanity gives.

Holler for Guidance

Although human beings have the understated superpowers of intuition and predictive causal thought, this isn't to say anyone has all the answers. Sadly, the species has not (yet) evolved to that point where you can bat a thousand all the time, making all of your decisions foolproof and your life easy-peasy. Instead, everyone is simply bobbing about in the puddle of human experience, trying to keep their head above water and hoping for the best!

In times of intense stress, grief, and turmoil, the very human response is typically to look for guidance anywhere and everywhere you can. After all, who wants to feel like they're swimming alone? This tendency has formed the basis of religions and explains the important role of spirituality and mysticism throughout human history. Never satisfied to simply *not* have the answers, the human animal looks outside the realm of the mundane for sources of divine guidance.

Although religion and spirituality are certainly not as present in the modern world as they once were, that doesn't mean the desire or need for some sort of outer guidance doesn't remain. Something very deep within the human psyche longs to seek answers, to turn toward the unknown for support from the subtle realms. Some still look for answers in religion, while others seek it in tarot cards, reading the clouds, or looking for signs from the Universe. There is a very human urge to holler into the void to request guidance, and this is something that even the most hard-core modern atheist may turn to in times of intense difficulty and stress. Armed with the knowledge that this is a part of your nature, you can find some feral self-care in approaching this in a purposeful and intentional way.

So shuck off the conditioning that would have you struggle alone and lean into the desire to holler for guidance—whatever that might look like for you.

How to Do It

The next time you're experiencing a problem or situation that feels just too difficult to cope with alone, allow yourself to channel that very human urge to ask for divine guidance. This does not need to be a "religious" or New Agey act either (unless you want it to be). It can be more an act of release and openness. An act of giving yourself permission to lean into the human urge to holler into the void in hopes it hollers back! Whether this be to God, the Universe, the burnt image of Mary Magdalene on toast, your ancestors, or even to a fictional character or archetype, such as Cthulhu or the jester, the *who* doesn't matter so much as the *why*. And the "why" is to surrender and simply allow yourself to fulfill the need to cry, "Jesus (or whoever), come take the wheel!"

Commune with a Flame

Throughout human history, people have been aided by fire. It is used for warmth, for cooking, for light, and for countless other things that have made it of indisputable benefit. The ability to wield fire, to invoke it, and to direct its use is one that sets humans apart, changing the trajectory of the species and allowing people to survive *and* thrive in a multitude of ways.

According to the myths and lore of the Greeks, human beings first received the gift of fire from the Titan god Prometheus, who stole it from the gods (and subsequently paid dearly for this theft). According to science—well, there've been many theories of how people began to work with and yield fire. The important role it plays in individual lives and cultures makes the origin story a compelling question. However, the one thing you can know for certain is that the ability to control fire has shifted life in unquestionably significant ways.

The importance of fire is not only limited to its role in mundane tasks. The presence of fire has a deeper, more spiritual role in human culture and society as well. To commune with a fire has been an integral part of social life, with humans gathering around the flames telling stories, keeping warm, and feasting together throughout time. On a spiritual level, fire (one of the core elements along with earth, air, and water) has been a mainstay in ritual, ceremony, and private practice. Even in modern times these uses remain, with the fire fulfilling a special role as a space to gather, to worship, and to feel fundamentally and primally human.

So if you want to feel primally and spiritually connected as a human being, find some feral self-care by communing with a flame. Whether this be gathering fireside in a group, solitarily gazing into a flame, or cooking food over its warmth, to bond with a flame is a deeply fulfilling and fundamentally human act.

How to Do It

To commune with a fire depends on what you have available. If you have access to a space where you can have a proper campfire/bonfire, such as a fire pit or fire bowl, grab some chairs and go sit fireside when it is dark outside. If you are able to do this socially, you can have some drinks and snacks, put on some music, and tell stories as you enjoy the flames together. If you are doing this alone, you can set yourself up comfortably to gaze into the flames as a meditative practice. Feel free to also look at the stars or howl at the moon to boost the feral self-care benefits!

If you do not have access to a larger flame, feel free to commune with a candle. Candles in jars are a great option for those who are clumsy and accident-prone (just make sure you never leave a flame unattended). To commune with a candle, simply light it and gaze at the flame. Breathe, relax, and enjoy the fiery show as it flickers and dances.

Honor Someone or Something Lost

Some of the earliest evidence of humans are burial sites, which show the reverence for the dead that the species holds. Death is one of life's true mysteries; as one of the only guarantees of life, it is both morbid and fascinating. Entire belief systems have been built around this great puzzle, and the looming threat of it influences lifestyles, choices made, and approaches to life in general.

Earlier in this book you explored the enormity of grief. This is not exclusive to humans either; you can find the awareness of death in other species, most notably primate kin. There have been documented cases of primate mothers continuing to carry their infants who have passed, and other cases where behavior similar to grief or sadness (including lethargic affect) has been witnessed in our primate relatives.

Given both the certainty of death and the enormity of grief, humans are left to cope with the loss of loved ones in the best ways they know how. You do this instinctively and intuitively in whichever way feels right in the moment, whether it be ritual, prayer, art, discussion of the person's life, or simply basking in the memories of that lost person. To honor the life of someone lost also honors human nature, giving you the space to get hands-on with your grief. This is an act of feral self-care that can help you both remember and move on. In honoring the loss, you do not lose the connection. Instead, that love remains, and the light that that person or thing brought to your world becomes a flame that your remembrance can keep stoked in perpetuity.

So when you find yourself faced with a loss, whether it be a person or even the death of something that was important to you, like a dream or a piece of your identity, create space to honor the place this person or thing held in your life.

How to Do It

If you are struggling with the loss of someone or something that was important to you, create a sacred circle for your grief. This circle may be in the form of a ritual that honors what was lost, a physical space such as an altar that is devoted to their remembrance, or simply giving yourself a special time and place to reflect on the impact this person or thing made on your life.

Lean into what feels intuitively right as a way to honor them. In taking the time and space to do so, you are also honoring your own grief and giving yourself the gift of working through the messy human experience of loss.

Find Meaning and Purpose

When operating your human vessel, it's important to remember that it definitely works best when given a meaning and a purpose. Along with this big brain you have, you also have big needs for pointing your intentions in directions that are significant. After all, should you not align yourself with meaning and purpose, the tendency to seek these things can be hijacked and used against you!

Modern humanity seems to be stuck at a strange intersection where there is so much convenience, security, and safety, and yet many struggle significantly in the realm of happiness and life satisfaction. Although there are many varied reasons for this, it's possible that you might be having a crisis of purpose. With life becoming easier (in the survival sense) with technological advances and convenience culture, and spirituality being pushed to the fringe, the context for finding meaning is drastically different than it was for your ancestors. While your ancestors may have found meaning and purpose in things like survival, rituals, and community-building for the good of the group, those things look a little different in the present tense.

It's important to remember that no matter how it may feel in the moment, especially if you are in the depths of depression or are swimming in the feeling of aimlessness, there is purpose and meaning woven throughout your life. It is there even when you feel like you can't quite grasp it. You get glimmers of this when you sink into gratitude, when you reach out and help another, and when you find the things in your life that light you up.

There is truly meaning and purpose all around you; sometimes it's just a matter of something shifting *within* you in order to see it better. In many cases this requires some examination and reflection: What are the underlying values and belief systems you have that govern your behavior and your perceptions? How can these values and systems help you find meaning and thrive?

Having a clear sense of your values, beliefs, desires, and goals is fundamental to really being able to suss out how you do life—and why. These are the things that drive you and the moves you make in a purposeful and meaningful way. The following feral self-care activity will help you explore your own values, beliefs, desires, and goals.

How to Do It

1. Grab a notebook and a pen and begin to write out a list of your core values. These are the fundamental principles that guide and dictate your life, behavior, and actions. For example, things like honesty, compassion, or loyalty may be core values for you. Once you've figured out your values, ask yourself how these values play out in your life. How have they been challenged and reaffirmed?

2. Once you have your list of values, you can further explore how these show up in a meaningful way in your life by making a series of values statements. These are statements of intent that affirm what your core values are and how they may be expressed. Try to make these statements kind of quippy and silly, as it's a fun and creative way to tackle serious business with levity. Some examples:

   • "Be a loyal bitch unless there's reason to be otherwise."
   • "Find balance between kindness and honesty."
   • "Love others even when they're being jerks."
   • "Live each day with purpose (this may include naps)."
   • "Focus on community over competition, capiche?"

3. Once you've created these statements, store them in your journal and revisit them frequently, or alternatively, put them up on little sticky notes that you can see often.

Find Comfort in Surrender

Starting with the first chapter and moving throughout this book, you've explored the concept of weaving chaos. As a modern human being, it's easy to act under the assumption and illusion that you are in control. And yes, there are a great many things modern humans in the Western world *do* have control over in comparison to early hunter-gatherers. However, the truth is that you still live in the shadow of the chaos of the natural world.

Life itself is full of twists and turns; it's got shifty trickster energy, as your best laid plans can be razed in an instant by one of the many variables that pepper your existence. To be alive is to navigate this chaotic soup. Ultimately, a spiritual surrender to the complex mysteries of what is to come is required.

Although modern culture tends to tell you that self-care can be found in things that are bought and sold, in reality it is all around you and can be found in unexpected ways, such as how you approach life. Sometimes self-care is acknowledging when to let go and recognizing that the messy business of life is inherently chaotic and unpredictable. If life did come with a handbook, you may find this straight in the introduction: "Learn to let go, or proceed at your own peril..."

So your feral self-care task is simply this: Find peace in not knowing, in not being able to predict or control the way things are going to go. This is a form of faith for the rational age. Let go and fly with only the unknown as your copilot, much like you would those final moments as you spring off a diving board or as you raise your arms on the stomach-churning drops of a roller coaster. Your life is the ride, and the mystery is the magic!

How to Do It

Create a surrender strategy that you can use when you find yourself in a place of trying to make sure everything will go "just right." Some examples of surrender strategies are:

- Affirming to yourself, "Perhaps I'll find peace in letting this shit go."
- Sitting in a warm bath and reflecting on all the times plans went sideways and you still ended up okay.
- Screaming into a pillow and then taking a deep, refreshed breath.
- Writing down all the bad things that will happen if things don't go your way, then shrugging your shoulders and telling yourself it's all gonna be okay.
- Making a list in your journal of all the times things didn't go your way but went in an even better, unexpected direction.

Whenever you begin to notice yourself obsessing about something going the way you want it to, stop and take a few deep breaths, then use your chosen surrender strategy. And always, always, always just know that no matter what, things are going to be okay in the end. Even when they're not okay in the moment, eventually they will be.

Direct Your Own Reality

Throughout this book you've explored the immense power of manifesting your reality through the imagination space. As a spiritual being, this is a concept that is juicy and compelling. It posits that you can be an active co-creator of your life through your thoughts, beliefs, and feelings. More importantly though, it's a system of belief that acknowledges the immense power of your subconscious self-concepts over what you experience as reality.

Now, since many manifestation-based belief systems can devolve into toxic rhetoric that victim blames (such as the insane notion that you are somehow making yourself sick or creating negative circumstances through "bad" thoughts) and bypasses the value and importance of *all* states of emotion and feeling (yes, even "negative vibes" have value and purpose), the word can be a trigger for some. However, the premise that your thoughts can influence your reality is actually pretty solid and has some psychological merit. Research shows that your attitudes and belief systems can have a huge impact on how you interpret, and thereby experience, life. How does this factor in when trying to make reality your bitch? Well, if you think something is impossible, then chances are you will act in a way that will continue to keep that thing off-limits for you. Whereas if you believe that you can make things happen, you will be more likely to try and do just that!

Recognizing the immense influence of thought and beliefs over how you interpret and experience life can be a truly empowering thing. From a feral self-care perspective, it allows you to tap into the spiritual realm while still working with your own human psychology in order to step into your abilities and break the barriers of what you believe is true and possible.

By allowing your mind to approach the concept of reality co-creation from a place of curiosity and play (rather than logic or rationalism), you can ease into a place where life feels more expansive and less scary. So take some time to entertain "impossible" dreams. You may find yourself more in control and open to possibility than you ever believed!

How to Do It

Take a mental inventory of something in your life that you want to see shift. Pick something that would have the most significant impact (for example, improving self-confidence or building a better social life), and try and imagine what those circumstances being shifted would actually look and feel like. Ask yourself if it feels like this is something that is a possible outcome for you. If the answer is no, then ask yourself why. Really explore this question, as much of the time you may feel restricted by beliefs that are not actually true.

When reflecting on what you want to shift, start affirming to yourself that it can be a possibility for you. Roll the idea over in your mind until you begin to feel more comfortable with it as being the outcome. If need be, affirm to yourself just how likely this shift will be for you.

The key to this practice is clarity. The more clarity you have as to what you want your end state to look and feel like, the more likely you will be able to achieve what you want. After all, the core of making things happen is just as rooted in your belief systems as it is in your actions. If you hold your goals and your desires in the forefront of your awareness, you are very much more likely to take the steps required to bring them into fruition!

Find Your Flow State

By now it's pretty much a well-established fact that meditation is good for you. Research shows that it increases positive feelings and the ability to manage stress, depression, and anxiety. Furthermore, meditating on a regular basis can also have physiological benefits, such as boosting immunity and reducing the likelihood of illness and disease. However, like most things that are good for you, it can feel borderline impossible! Indeed, the idea of "thinking nothing" can seem so completely outside the realm of possibility for the average person, that it almost makes meditation itself seem like some sort of mythical ideal. Like a unicorn or an honest politician!

But the trust is that meditation is not really as complicated as it's been made out to be. Despite the prevailing idea that meditation is "thinking nothing," really it is about being so present in the experience of the current moment that you are able to reach beyond the incessant chatter of the brain. Thoughts may still pop up, but they won't be in control of you.

For the incessantly thinking human mammal, to give yourself the gift of meditation is a deeply restoring act of feral self-care. Not just because your creature body needs a break from the mental chaos that you spend so much of your time, energy, and awareness on. But also because it is a divine act of love and kindness to allow yourself to engage in something that has such clear wellness and health benefits. To do so is an utter rejection of the modern societal notions that make people martyr their mental health on the altar of productivity. This is powerful stuff.

If you have struggled to meditate in the past, it may be helpful to take "meditation" straight out of the equation. The word itself has become a trigger and can act as a catalyst for failure. Instead, I ask you this: What is your flow-state activity? By this I mean: What is the thing that sets you alight and gives your brain the space it needs to pause? The activity that puts you in a state of peaceful flow? For some it is running. For others, it is playing a musical instrument, such as a piano or guitar. Everyone has *something* that moves them to a space of calm and measured awareness where the ever-sucking spiral of the mental vortex and all its associated anxieties can't find them.

Your feral self-care assignment is to figure out your own flow-state activity.

How to Do It

1. Chances are as you read the previous sentences your mind will have already drifted off to what your flow-state activity is. Scribble it here on the page or say it aloud.
2. Think for a moment on why you chose this activity. What does that flow state feel like when you enjoy this practice? How is this flow state different than your regular state? What about this activity made it pop into your head?
3. Now ask yourself: "How often do I engage in this activity?" It's typically considered ideal if people can engage in meditation at least once a day. Do you hit this mark with your flow-state activity, or do you fall short?
4. Reflect on how you could start using it more or whether there are similar activities that can help you mimic this state.

Vibe in a Sacred Space

Sites of early humans are fascinating. In these places, you can learn a lot about how your ancestors lived, the things that were important to them, and the way they interacted with the world around them. Some of the more fascinating sites are the sacred ones. Sacred sites are places that are considered holy or otherworldly in a divine sense, and the role they typically play in human culture is being a space of worship or reverent importance. While sacred sites in the archaeological sense are ones with evidence of past use, sacred spaces are all around you, even where there isn't necessarily an artifact to dig up.

There are a variety of cues that a space is sacred. Some sacred sites are considered such based on particular environmental features (mountains, proximity to other landmarks, etc.) or how they align with the cosmos (constellations, sunrises, etc.). While others simply have an otherworldly "frequency" (energy) that is indescribably but undeniably present. Some are sacred because they were deliberately intended as such, such as built structures like churches and monuments. In any and all cases, you feel the presence of something beyond the veil of the ordinary. You are both humbled and in awe. Maybe you thought of a space that fits this description that isn't ancient at all—in fact, it may be a place you have access to wherever you live.

As a spiritually connected being, you can deliberately create sacred spaces as well. This is your birthright and a primal part of embracing your animal nature. You do not need organized religion or any sort of initiation to a specific spiritual tradition in order to create sacred space. All it takes is to be tapped into this dimension of your humanity!

So, carve out a little piece of feral self-care by intentionally playing with the concept of sacred space and inviting it into your life. To do so is to fulfill a primal need, transcending the ordinary to connect to something divine.

How to Do It

If you have already found a place that feels sacred, visit it often and simply allow yourself to be present there. Modern-day spirituality can feel very performative at times, but fundamentally, all you truly need to do is go bask in the presence of the divine that is in and all around you. Be charged by the essence of simply vibing in this place.

If you are creating your own sacred space, like a small corner of your yard that you would like to fulfill this purpose, you can approach this with discipline and intention. What can you do to make this space feel sacred? Will you tend to it differently? Will you nourish it with gifts of song and stories? What things would you collect/display there to make it feel divine? Have fun creating something sacred all for yourself.

Craft a Ritual

Upon hearing the word "ritual," the mind can delight in wandering to pictures of ceremony, esoteric rites, hunched whispers, and solemn tones. But a ritual can be many things and can even be pulled out of the everyday minutiae of mundane life. This is because a ritual is a *tool*. It is something that emerges in even the most secular expressions of society as a way for you to create stability, predictability, and meaning.

A ritual is typically defined as a series of prescribed actions that are done in a specific, repeatable way. They can be ceremonial in nature; however, you can see the whisper of ritual in everything from skincare routines to eating habits. Beyond the individual, human society tends to incorporate ritual as a way of marking serious or important things. For example, customs of "ribbon cutting" ceremonies or the persistence of "swearing oaths" in the legal system. The thing about rituals, even in the seemingly nonspiritual and ordinary corners of life, is that they can make things *feel* important, lending a potent sense of meaning and purpose to your activities.

Throughout this chapter, you've explored the importance of the spiritual dimension in this messy business of being alive. Humans are spiritual beings, and as such, you crave the order and transcendence that ritual provides. By finding opportunities to invite ritual (and the sense of reverent meaning that comes with) into your life, you can get a quick burst of self-care that nourishes this aspect of your humanity. This also allows you to provide yourself with stability and routine— welcome structures in a life experience that can often feel fraught with fuckery and completely out of your control.

Rituals can help you sink more deeply into the experience of your life. *You* are the occasion. *Being alive* is the ceremony. Give yourself some feral self-care by inviting ritual, allowing little pockets of magic to seep into the daily grind.

How to Do It

Pick something in your life that you want to ritualize. Some examples would be:

- A cleaning routine (such as cleaning your kitchen at the end of the night).
- A personal care routine (such as shaving your legs).
- A morning routine of planning out your day.
- Taking your dog for a walk every afternoon or evening.

Now think of the steps required to actually do this task and break them up into a discrete order. Next, think of some elements you can add to this routine to make it a more vibey experience. For example, lighting candles, using specific playlists, pairing the routine with mantras or affirmations—whatever you would like. This is not just a way to build a ritual but to *enhance your experience* of doing the ritual.

As a self-care bonus, ritualizing tasks makes them more likely to be completed. Whether it is a subconscious desire to give these rituals the reverence they deserve or that you are simply more mindful as a side effect of having routines become an "experience," rituals help you succeed while also making life feel more vibey and fun.

About the Author

MANDI EM is an author and chaotic wellness witch. She's the author of *Witchcraft Therapy* and *Happy Witch*, and she shares funny, approachable self-help guidance on her blog and social channels at *Healing for Hot Messes*, along with resources for nonreligious witches over at *The Secular Witch*. Her writing has been featured in *The New York Times*, *HuffPost*, *SheKnows*, *Refinery29*, *McSweeney's*, and more. She and her husband are born-again hippies raising their three children in beautiful Vernon, British Columbia, in Canada.